BÔ YIN RÂ
(JOSEPH ANTON SCHNEIDERFRANKEN)

VOLUME 14
OF THE 32-VOLUME CYCLE
THE GATED GARDEN

THE PATH OF MY PUPILS

For information
about the books of Bô Yin Râ and
titles available in English translation,
visit the Kober Press web site at
http://www.kober.com.

THE KOBER PRESS PUBLISHES THE ONLY ENGLISH TRANSLATIONS
OF THE BOOKS OF BÔ YIN RÂ AUTHORIZED BY THE KOBER VERLAG,
SWITZERLAND. THE KOBER VERLAG PUBLISHES THE BOOKS OF
BÔ YIN RÂ IN THE ORIGINAL GERMAN AND HAS PROTECTED
THEIR INTEGRITY SINCE THE AUTHOR'S LIFETIME.

BÔ YIN RÂ
(JOSEPH ANTON
SCHNEIDERFRANKEN)

THE PATH OF MY PUPILS

TRANSLATED FROM THE GERMAN
BY JAN SCHYMURA, MALKA WEITMAN
AND ERIC STRAUSS

BERKELEY, CALIFORNIA

Copyright ©2017 by Eric Strauss

Eric Strauss, Publisher & Editor

All rights reserved.

For permission to quote or excerpt, email:
koberpress@mindspring.com

This book is a translation from the German of *Der Weg meiner Schüler* by Bô Yin Râ (J.A. Schneiderfranken), published in 1932 by Kober'sche Verlagsbuchhandlung, Basel-Leipzig. The copyright to the German text is held by Kober Verlag AG, Bern, Switzerland.

Printed in the United States of America

International Standard Book Number: 978-0-915034-30-7

Typography and composition by Dickie Magidoff

Book cover after a design by Bô Yin Râ

CONTENTS

1 Who Do I Consider to Be My Pupils? . 7
2 A Necessary Distinction 23
3 Needless Self-Torment. 45
4 Unavoidable Difficulties 61
5 Dynamic Faith. 81
6 The Greatest Obstacle 93
7 Pupils and their Companions. 105
8 Inner Life and Outer World 125
9 How One Ought to Use My Books . . 153

CHAPTER ONE

WHO DO I CONSIDER TO BE MY PUPILS?

I CERTAINLY CANNOT CALL ALL WHO CONSIDER themselves as such to be my pupils. However, those who have proven themselves to be on the path through their conduct and deeds, and those who feel the inner readiness to pursue it, though they have not yet begun the journey, do not need my acknowledgement in order to be my pupils.

Here all are their own judge and jury.

Judges over themselves, whose judgments cannot be appealed for all Eternity.

Such judgments are not based on an external code of law but, rather, on the effect our actions have upon our inner life.

Each of us shapes our inner being through our conduct in the world and the truth of who we are is none other than what our conduct shows us to be.

We may indulge ourselves by believing the attractive self-image that we see in the mirror of our mind and fool others with the pleasing persona we exhibit to the world, but this does not change by one iota our position in the realm of radiant Spirit, which is determined solely by our actions.

Those who truly are my pupils know themselves to be so, because they act in the way my teachings would have my pupils act.

They do not need me to acknowledge them as such because their own conduct gives them all the inner confirmation that they need.

I cannot *make* even a single human being into a pupil of mine; I cannot turn anyone into a person united with me within the primordial light of the Spirit. Those who dedicate their thoughts, feelings, intention, speech and deeds towards pursuing the path I describe become so of their own making.

Whether or not my pupils know me personally is of no significance for their own inner progress.

WHO DO I CONSIDER TO BE MY PUPILS?

This mortal, flawed body of mine, afflicted by a multitude of ailments—the physical body in which I dwell on this earth—is no more to me in this visible realm than what the visible hands of a clock are to the mechanism hidden within.

With regard to the teachings I offer, my physical body is merely the intermediary.

It is also of no consequence when people claim —in an embarrassingly clichéd way—to be my "disciples" simply because they have read my books. Reading the words I have written does not, in itself, make someone a pupil of mine.

If my words have only been absorbed through the *mind*, they are merely a mental possession, and will only be retained so long as one's mental faculties are intact.

Nothing of it will endure!

Only that which has been put into practice in daily life, and has thereby taken form in inner life, shall endure—even after not a single atom of the brain still exists in the state once needed to grasp my teachings.

One does not become my pupil as a result of a distinction I "award."

All those who have delved into my teachings and who have committed themselves to live their lives in accordance with them, may rightfully consider themselves to be pupils of mine.

My personal contribution is limited to the fact that I have put into words my own experiences and have become the interpreter of ancient teachings of Truth that I have been privileged to put to the test.

To be sure, we are dealing with realms of experience that are wholly inaccessible to my fellow human beings on the western side of the globe and accessible to only a vanishing few on the other, none of whom have been charged with the task of presenting these sacred teachings to the public.

WHO DO I CONSIDER TO BE MY PUPILS?

I CANNOT FORBID any of my pupils from calling me their "master" since it is commonly known that in the Orient, individuals of my kind and, for that matter, other kinds of spiritual teachers, are referred to by titles that convey this concept. There may indeed be justification, within the realm of Spirit, for addressing me by this term. However, it only has meaning and worth to me if those who use such honorifics understand the deep reality they connote.

Very few individuals are able to use these words with an understanding of their full meaning. Therefore, I ask that I not be called "master": No one becomes my pupil and enters into spiritual relationship with me by describing or addressing me in this way.

It is foolish to believe that a relationship that reaches far beyond this earthly existence and is rooted in the realm of pure Spirit would depend upon some external form of recognition.

THERE ARE those who, with best of intentions, take it upon themselves to send me every favorable review of my books that appears in the press, thinking it will bring me joy, and to write me veritable condolence letters in an attempt to console me every time some small-time columnists in newspapers, read only in the local pub, indulge their need to impress their readers—not one of whom will likely ever become my pupil—with crude wit and caustic comments. Such gestures reveal their incorrect understanding of my role as teacher and as spiritual guide.

I generally regard reviewers in magazines and newspapers of substance with respect, giving them the credit due to fellow human beings who have well thought-out opinions.

One can usually tell from the very first sentence with "what manner of spirit" a reviewer is imbued and how seriously their opinions should be considered, without even knowing their name or nom de plume.

Were I writing poetry or scientific works I would look upon the critiques of competent reviewers as reflections on my work which might be useful to me in the future, and would therefore consider their opinions to be of considerable importance and feel obliged to study them.

WHO DO I CONSIDER TO BE MY PUPILS?

But I do not present myself to the public as a scientist or poet, or a representative of a religious body. My teachings derive directly from my individual experiences and a capacity for a quality of perception that has been granted to me, which no other person in Europe currently possesses. Thus, it is difficult for even the most well-intentioned of reviewers to evaluate the texts I have felt obliged to write, and their critiques are of little use to me. On the other hand, such reviews may be of great help in placing my books in the hands of those who are still searching and in need of them.

Those serious reviewers whose words have led to a wider dissemination of my books understand better than anyone that my books can only be truly judged by one who is already guided by them in daily life.

Lastly, it is hardly worth mentioning the absurdly mistaken ways in which my writings are classified and my person labeled, in many of the letters I receive—some amusing, some arrogant—and to which I shall never be able to reply.

THE PATH OF MY PUPILS

THIS SEEMS the place to explicitly state that I am unable to engage in regular correspondence with even my most dedicated students. So if I do not answer a particular letter, my silence should not be taken as a negative comment on the letter or its writer—as is implied in the popular saying "no answer is also an answer."

A particular letter may interest me intensely or call forth in me a burning empathy; there may be much I wish to comment on—and yet I must refrain. I have long ago reached the limits of my circle of correspondence and can barely maintain it, let alone extend its radius. I must conserve my energies and guard them from becoming fragmented so that I may devote myself to the principal tasks entrusted to me for my lifetime; tasks which demand the deepest, inner concentration.

Those pupils closest to me have the insight to understand and respect my position, without my having to explain it. And many who are further removed from me share the same understanding, as is evidenced by the many letters I receive from writers who simply convey warm, heartfelt greetings, and often do not even include a return address.

To them I extend my sincerest thanks!

※

I MUST EMPHATICALLY counter a misconception about the obligations of my pupils which, unfortunately, is held by some who are otherwise quite admirable and far advanced.

I am referring to attempts to proselytize; that is, the desire to become a kind of "missionary" who seeks converts to my teachings and holds oneself out as an "apostle."

Nothing has impeded my work as much as this type of misguided zeal on the part of my faithful pupils. Nothing could be more detrimental to or interfere more with the ability to thoughtfully and soberly assimilate my teachings.

I understand the good intentions behind such efforts and am aware of the motivations that lead to such excessive zeal. To those who seek so eagerly to speed the dissemination of my books I would say that, ironically, their efforts turn more people away from an openness to my teaching than lead them to it.

Those who give in to such missionary fervor slightly overestimate their ability to persuade others, and grossly underestimate the power of the primordial, spiritual forces, which guide my life-task and its ultimate impact.

Experience has shown me that among those I consider to be my true spiritual pupils only a handful first heard of my books from a proselytizing pupil. Most were led to my books in serendipitous or sometimes strange ways—the books simply "came" to them. This has been the case even with rather worldly individuals who had no intention of pursuing spiritual matters.

⁂

Some of my pupils seem to overlook the difference between their well-meaning proselytizing and the strategies publishers use to market their books. However, there is a fundamental difference between them.

When zealous pupils "market" my books, they take it upon themselves to decide who might become a future pupil of mine; whereas, my publisher markets my books to the general public, thus leaving the decision of who

WHO DO I CONSIDER TO BE MY PUPILS?

will be led to my books to the spiritual guidance of each individual.

My publisher's marketing campaign is based on the premise that there are many potential readers who might be in urgent need of my books, but are as yet unaware of their existence. Thus, my publisher aims its advertising at the broadest potential audience and readers find their way to my books by a process of self-selection—a sifting of souls that is guided from the Spirit's realm and which never errs.

I<small>N CONTRAST</small>, even the most well-intentioned attempt by one individual to persuade another is—with rare exceptions—an intrusion into a fellow human being's personal sphere and an encroachment upon their autonomy.

Such unsolicited efforts may have unintended negative results: An individual who is not yet ready for my books, although my zealous pupil thinks otherwise, may feel pressured and develop an aversion to them. Beyond this, one should remember that many people only value that which they have discovered for themselves.

THE PATH OF MY PUPILS

The very persons who now feel distanced from my books might in a few days or weeks have found them on their own. But now, because of the pressure placed on them, months or years may have to pass before they feel open to encountering them once more.

I can, unfortunately, recall all too many instances in which an over-eager pupil tried to win readers to my books only to be met with anger and resistance. Some of these unfortunate victims of misplaced zeal have eventually found their way to my books nonetheless, only to tell me later what befell them.

Those who wish to act correctly and with wisdom would do well to trust the powers of the Spirit's realm, in whose care my books are held, to direct my words to those readers who are ready to receive them.

I do not mean to imply that one should avoid speaking of my books; I only ask that readers refrain from trying to persuade others and gain "converts" to my teachings.

My most accomplished pupils are usually the very ones who feel compelled to champion to others that which has brought illumination to themselves. My remarks, therefore, are directed most particularly to them.

⚛

I MUST ALSO caution each and every one of my pupils not to demand too much of themselves or of their fellow pupils.

As a conscientious guardian of the path on which my pupils will be led into the Spirit's realm and thereby find the sure knowledge of their own place there, I have cleared away a multitude of obstacles that would have otherwise required superhuman effort to overcome.

However, it is not possible for me to level every incline on the path for, by its very by nature, it must traverse the steepest cliffs— and can be mastered only with the greatest perseverance.

I cannot spare any of my pupils the toil and struggle of the climb, nor can I carry any of them to the summit on my shoulders.

Each steep rise can best be mastered if climbers pace themselves and use their strength wisely and with moderation, and thus avoid the dangers of exhaustion.

Impatient souls may be fooled into thinking they can speed their way by struggling to make progress. But quiet confidence and unwavering faith in one's own inner strength will more readily lead those who seek the Spirit to their sublime goal than any straining of the will.

CHAPTER TWO

A NECESSARY DISTINCTION

In this chapter, BYR discusses the way in which he wishes the German word Geist *to be understood. In German,* Geist *can refer to either the spirit or the intellect, depending upon context. Thus, this chapter deals with a problem of meaning that does not occur in English. If English-speaking readers keep this in mind, they will find that this chapter, nevertheless, has much to offer them.* —the editors

It should be clear from all my books how I wish the word *Geist* to be understood.

However, because in everyday usage and in scholarly terminology the word *Geist* is often used to describe mental activity and all the creativity that flows from it, I note that some of my pupils habitually misinterpret the word when they encounter it in my books.

This confusion is by no means surprising since in everyday parlance the word *Geist* can refer to either intellectual or spiritual work, or a state of either spiritual or mental freshness or fatigue. One may say that someone's speech is *geistvoll*, that is, eloquent, or that their *Geist* has become plunged into night, that is, deranged. Some believe that at its highest *Geist* refers to intellect, and seat this meaning upon a throne of honor, while others declare war on this interpretation and seek to overthrow it, and elevate the soul instead.

Most commonly, the word *Geist* is used to describe mental activity—innate functions of the brain that have become perfected through use, or mental agility and stamina. One may also refer to illnesses of *Geist*, but these are actually disregulations of the *brain*—mental illnesses—which may arise from identifiable physical causes or through influences of an occult nature.

When human beings confuse the meanings of *Geist*—so that, for example, they speak of a "lively spirit" when they actually mean a "lively mind"—it is a sign of their remoteness from the spirit, of how very far they have fallen from conscious Being in the realm of radiant Spirit.

※

I<small>N SOME INSTANCES</small> the word *Geist* is used to refer to a disembodied being—a manifestation from life beyond that is generally invisible to human eyes—and here we can detect a last, lingering remembrance of our primordial existence within the realm of radiant Spirit. This is true even though the images human beings create to make the unseen realm concrete and comprehensible to themselves are, at times, grotesque, fantastical and tasteless.

In Europeanized cultures and religions, the word *Geist* is often used to mean spirit and much is said about it. However, if one listens closely to the tone and feeling of the speakers one soon realizes that what is being described is still a kind of *mental* perception, albeit of a very subtle type—even when they are discussing such sacred subjects as "the Spirit of Eternity," "the Spirit of God" or "the Holy Spirit."

Indeed, God is Spirit and "they that worship Him must worship Him in spirit" and thus "in truth." And yet this spirit, which is God, is often only understood to be a most sublime experience of the *mind*, and, therefore, worshiping in spirit is held to be no different than worshiping in thought.

No one remembers that there exists a timeless Spirit whose radiance alone is able to illuminate our inner life such that we may comprehend the Living God within our very selves.

It should come as no surprise when battle cries are raised against those who are so dazzled by the feats and insights of which the mind is capable that they consider the intellect—*Geist* in its meaning as mind—to reign supreme.

No wonder that one should seek to defend the *Geist* of the soul against the *Geist* of the mind!

One feels impelled to take a stand out of an inner certainty that this worldly *Geist* of the mind cannot be the highest and the best we may experience.

One feels one's way through darkness using inner senses and tries to near the soul. Within the soul one feels a power that is infinite and great, surpassing any consciousness of self the brain may bring about.

"The spirit searcheth all things, yea, the deep things of God." These words of Paul cease to have meaning if one believes the spirit is no more than something generated by brain cells.

What is being spoken of here is the radiant, eternal Spirit, which in no way depends upon the brain and which, in fact, *creates* the brain out of itself. All this has, sadly, long ago receded into secret knowledge.

HUMAN BEINGS have given themselves over to ever more complex intellectual pursuits; they have fallen under a spell, seduced by the erroneous belief that thought, which is dependent upon the brain, is of the timeless Spirit. Very few among them have preserved the understanding that there is a kind of knowledge that can never be attained by reason, analysis or thought—a kind of knowledge that comes through *felt experience* of Spirit.

Hardly anyone remains who can tell how one might gain this kind of knowledge, despite the many testimonies we have that such a thing is possible.

Such a thing has only ever been possible for those who had entered fully into the Spirit: those who had become fully conscious of the immutable, indestructible radiant Spirit of Eternity, that is itself the source of its own life.

※

THIS SPIRIT cannot be grasped with the brain's thoughts nor with the body's senses.

We must enter "into" the Spirit if we wish to perceive, fathom, or probe into the Spirit's realm. And it is indeed possible to enter into the Spirit because we are permeated by Spirit, even throughout our physical bodies: the Spirit lives in us even if we are not yet able to live in the Spirit.

However, we can never become conscious of the Spirit through mental activity.

We are dealing here with something palpable, that actually takes place, not with an abstraction or a product of imagination.

A NECESSARY DISTINCTION

This experience can be registered by the brain and then take shape in the mind as thought—but it is impossible for the mind to bring it about.

THE PATH TO such an experience is shown in my books.

I have written them in order to point out the necessary steps. Truly, all my heart and soul has gone into the writing of these books!

There are many ways to walk upon the path and so I describe the different methods one may pursue in order to reach the goal.

Every word I have written serves to illuminate this path that is known only to a few so that all who wish to walk on it can, with little effort, find the ways most suitable to their abilities. I do not simply mark the path but also make visible the vista as it appears from certain milestones and even from the final goal.

READERS ARE mistaken when they believe their abilities to be so limitless that they feel free to choose any of the methods I set forth without considering whether it is suitable to them, or to pursue several or all the methods at one time.

Every human being is born with a different disposition and different natural abilities and is further shaped from youth by relationships, circumstances and experiences, as well as by their own fixed ideas and the opinions of others. All these influences determine the methods best suited to that person in pursuing the path to the Spirit.

I believe I have clearly delineated the different considerations each individual should bear in mind when choosing which practices to follow.

OTHERS OF MY kind, who know just as I do the different ways the path may be pursued, but who have grown to spiritual maturity under the tutelage of Eastern teachers—whose unrelenting discipline seems to us severe and even cruel—nonetheless consider my writings to be all too easy to understand. They are of the opinion that the path to the Spirit can never have too few obstacles, for only those who remain undeterred even in the face of formidable challenges are worthy of the goal.

True initiates of the ancient mysteries of China, India, Babylonia, Persia, Egypt, Greece and Rome, all of which still had real knowledge of the possibilities for inner experience described in my books, agreed with this stern approach.

Readers should be aware that the clear and explicit manner in which I write is based on sound reasons. I am thus able to take full responsibility for my words.

To be sure, the decision to write in this straightforward way was mine, but I made it with full awareness of why this decision was left to me in particular.

I AM NOT A PERSON from ancient times nor am I of Asian origin although I encompass both these cultural spheres in time and space within my spiritual dimension. I am a European of the twentieth century—according to the calendar used in Christian countries—and as such I am only too familiar with the impatience that is characteristic of the people of my time. I know that very few of those who share this earthly life with me could hope to benefit from my teachings were I to write in cryptic language and create barriers to understanding that which I wish to make accessible to all.

And yet my writings deal with matters that do not lend themselves to language.

What I have to say is not easily expressed in words.

In addition, I do not have the benefit of a sufficiently prepared readership. Despite all the popularization of knowledge about bygone or non-western cultures, even scholars in these fields are not aware of the criteria needed to distinguish between superstition and true knowledge of reality.

Only those individuals who have already found their way into the realm of the Spirit and can therefore perceive from out of this consciousness possess the necessary discernment.

But such individuals can easily do without my books and I do not write for them.

A NECESSARY DISTINCTION

Those who wish to become my pupils because they are intent upon finding the path most suitable for them that will lead into consciousness of the Spirit will do well not to arbitrarily mingle the different approaches to pursuing the path. Rather, they should select the approach that speaks especially to them, and feel free to leave all other options aside.

I do not bring tidings of the radiant Spirit in order to impart a stern teaching that only the hardiest can follow.

From out of the Spirit, which is Love, I show the way of love and never-ending compassion—the way of boundless mercy.

Not only do I show the way, but also point out the distinguishing signposts that my pupils will benefit from recognizing.

Each person should heed the signposts most relevant to them and not allow themselves to be confused by those meant for others.

The word "Spirit," as I use it in my texts, has no earthly equivalent.

Spirit is the form in which primordial Being is expressed. All existence emanates from this primordial source and continues to draw life from it so long as that existence remains viable in the physical world.

Spirit can be compared to free-flowing electricity in a state of high tension that penetrates each material body within its force field and manifests in that body to the extent it is able to conduct such electricity. Although this is by no means an ideal comparison, it is nevertheless a useful image that may serve to prevent an erroneous understanding of what is meant by "Spirit."

Each of us carries within us the capacity to experience Spirit, this primal force that is the source of all Being. Without our conscious commitment, however, no amount of "grace" can allow this potential to unfold, so that the realm of radiant Spirit may become accessible to us.

❧

THIS WORLD OF timeless Spirit, encompassing within it countless other worlds—each one distinct unto itself—is neither fixed and rigid,

A NECESSARY DISTINCTION

nor is it without order and chaotic. It is a universe in constant motion, a cosmos of ever-changing forms that, for all their transformations, retain their pristine clarity and essence.

Those who would learn to experience the Spirit's realm within their being must first set aside their misconceptions. Most especially, they must set aside the mistaken idea that the Spirit, because it cannot be seen by mortal eyes, is in no way comparable to anything earthly senses can apprehend but is instead an ephemeral, free-floating state devoid of structured shapes and forms.

They must come to understand that Spirit is the ultimate source of their own life. Even while dwelling within a physical body, the Spirit's organism, the "body" of the Spirit, can awaken, and the Spirit's "senses" can unfold alongside the physical senses.

Those who search for inner Truth should also understand that the realm of Spirit can only be experienced through the spiritual senses, just as our familiar, physical world can only be experienced through our physical senses.

Furthermore, in the physical world, the quality of our experience is determined by the degree to which our physical senses are developed; so too, in the Spirit's realm, the depth of our experience is conditioned by our spiritual senses.

And just as in the material world each person will experience life differently, depending on the level to which his or her physical senses are developed and on which senses predominate, so also is each person's experience within the Spirit's world dependent on the particular ways in which the spiritual senses have unfolded, which is different for each spiritual entity.

※

To complete the analogy I am making, I must point out to my pupils yet another comparison that flows from those above, although it is by no means less important for understanding the nature of experience within the Spirit's world.

Here I am referring to the fact that we are able to behold both the material and the spiritual

A NECESSARY DISTINCTION

worlds with either cold objectivity and detachment or with all the warmth of our soul.

༄

W̲ʜᴇᴛʜᴇʀ ᴡᴇ ᴀʀᴇ experiencing material or spiritual reality using the physical or spiritual senses, we are only ever perceiving different aspects of the selfsame primal force. This force I have referred to in my books as "the only absolute Reality."

In all eternity, no consciousness can penetrate this absolute Reality other than that which is part of absolute Reality itself. Thus, absolute Reality would be impenetrable to even the most exalted levels of human spirits who dwell within the realm of Eternity—beings who exist at levels incomprehensible to mortal minds—were it not for the fact that absolute Reality, through its very existence, brings about certain energies of the soul—the soul forces—as a manifestation of its influence. Because these soul forces *derive from* absolute Reality, they are able to penetrate its consciousness. The soul forces are imbued with intentionality; they seek to be active in us in both the life of physical sensing and the life of spiritual sensing, unless we ourselves thwart this intention.

For this reason, it is essential that we be aware of which soul forces we endeavor to align with our will and integrate into our innermost being.

This awareness is essential not only for our time here on earth but, even more so, for our future existence in the realm of Eternity.

Those who wish to enter the sacred realm of the Spirit have a solemn obligation to protect their soul forces from harm, lest their noblest strivings lead inadvertently to the death of their soul. This is because a cold, objective approach to the Spirit, devoid of warmth and lacking in the depth of feeling that the soul provides, is nothing less than self-damnation; a curse that will not end until that consciousness has extinguished itself, in the course of aeons.

This is why all passionate defenders of the soul—even those who are far from true understanding of the timeless Spirit—are right to be concerned that the *Geist* of the mind not kill the life of the soul.

A NECESSARY DISTINCTION

The ability to experience the eternal realm differs wholly and completely from the skills involved in intellectual reasoning and thought—the *Geist* of the mind.

Here on this physical plane, however, where all experience is filtered through the physical senses, we need the mind and its abilities in order to reflect upon and communicate that which we experience in the realm of Spirit.

In contrast—if I may make an imprecise analogy—within the self that is formed of Spirit, the soul forces take the place of the physical brain, and it is these spiritual energies that give us the ability to experience the Eternal. Indeed, the life of the Spirit would not need to exist if we were not able to experience it; thus, the soul forces give the life of the Spirit its raison d'être.

I offer these explanations so as to make it easier for my pupils to shape their lives in accordance with the teachings in my books. Nonetheless, no one is more aware than I of the inadequacy of human language to convey spiritual reality.

THE PATH OF MY PUPILS

For this reason, I must ask that my pupils not engage in the cheap pleasure of exercising their undoubtedly keen intellects in trying to find interpretations to my words that are different than the one I have set forth.

The only way to convey something that must be *experienced* in order for it to be truly understood is indirectly, through the use of images, parables and metaphor.

I must take it as a given that my pupils have a sincere desire to understand my texts.

On the other hand, I cannot warn strongly enough against a rigid, cultish adherence to the literal meaning of my words.

Whoever wishes to be my pupil must learn to feel the *intended* meaning behind the words and act accordingly.

I certainly do not wish to establish a new kind of orthodoxy!

Each reader should feel free to translate my words into more personal and familiar language if doing so will facilitate understanding.

A NECESSARY DISTINCTION

As seekers advance on their path, they will have less need for images and metaphors, or any expressions of languages that exist to communicate matters of this world. Their own experience will, instead, serve as the sure footing for further progress on the path.

CHAPTER THREE

NEEDLESS SELF-TORMENT

Most people living in western cultures, regardless of which religion they espouse, are unaware of the potential for developing their spiritual organism so that it may truly be *experienced* and pervade their consciousness while they are still here on earth. This spiritual organism is *real* and is composed of spiritual substance—and it is this organism alone that is the carrier of consciousness after the death of the physical body.

Some may have heard of this potential, but often from questionable sources, and thus they are unable to believe it to be true.

Still others suspect that it may indeed be possible to know the world of the eternal Spirit—which cannot be apprehended through the physical senses—through direct experience.

They search in vain for a "method" that will help them attain such knowledge.

Because they know no other existence than the physical, many of these seekers conclude that they might reach the Spirit through the body. Thus, they believe that they will draw closer to the Spirit if they "purify" their bodies.

Although this poor, imperfect mortal body exists solely by virtue of the Spirit, it can never itself *become* Spirit.

One cannot help but realize that the body has its limits, and will resist when unreasonable demands are placed on it. Those who regard this resistance as a "weakness of the flesh" will then strive to "overcome" it and consider themselves victorious when they have deadened the very energies that have been granted to the mortal body by the Spirit, in order to enliven it.

Those who have been most severe in their self-denial—and therefore most "successful" in the "mortification of the flesh"—are now regarded as most spiritual.

They may experience hallucinations or other "acts of grace" which are taken to be proof of this delusion but are in truth nothing more than the consequences of torturing the body, in harsh or subtle ways, in violation of its nature and its needs.

Each religion has a history filled with accounts of such derangements of the senses and, unfortunately, with testimonials glorifying them.

One may admire the conviction of fellow human beings who practice self-mortification, but the inhumanity of what they do deserves no admiration.

We human beings on this earth are not meant to indulge our animal nature, or to be dominated by the drive for pleasure or the love of comfort. But neither should we deny the animal within us and subject it to abuse.

Rather, we should train our bodies to become an expression of the living Spirit that is our life force.

To this end, any method is more suitable and effective than mortification of the body.

I am not speaking as someone who has never practiced self-denial.

Many years ago, I too was of the opinion that fasting and other forms of self-denial were "pleasing to God." Not only did I observe the forty days of fasting leading up to Easter more strictly than a penitent monk, I also fasted at other times, abstaining from all nourishment, excepting spring water, for days at a time.

Others may be even more adept at such practices than I and I gladly acknowledge this. Once I awoke to conscious experience of the radiant, eternal Spirit I lost all desire to excel as an ascetic.

Since that time I know that the attraction to a life of asceticism is based in false thinking. There is only one justification for ascetic practices and that is when they are necessary as therapy and will therefore benefit the body.

I include here the inclination of certain individuals to lead a frugal or even Spartan way of life, when that life style is practiced for the

NEEDLESS SELF-TORMENT

purpose, whether real or perceived, of promoting health and physical well-being.

When asceticism is based on the belief that an ascetic life can lead one to the timeless Spirit, such practices become reprehensible indeed.

Whatever such athletes of asceticism consider to be spiritual experiences are, without exception, a cause for concern.

We are either dealing with the effects of a weakened physical body on the brain or else, it may be that the battered body has already fallen prey to occult forces from the invisible realm of the physical world. These forces will not of themselves let go of their pitiful victims but will instead seek to keep them "entertained," in whatever manner is most suitable, so as not to rouse the victims' critical faculties from slumber.

What the person so deceived takes to be a spiritual experience is in reality a state of nervous excitation and a ghostly spook caused by most unwelcome, animal-like creatures belonging to the physical realm—although they are invisible to the eye and cannot be detected by even the strongest microscope.

I have given very clear explanations in my books about the nature of these creatures, both their legitimate functions within the natural world as well as their aberrant behavior when stimulated by human beings.

Those who believe such matters to be trivial and unworthy of serious consideration do not suspect how many of their fellow humans are caught in the snares of these invisible, physical creatures.

Not only must I caution against asceticism and mortification of the body and its associated psychological dangers, but also against another kind of self-torment towards which many seekers are inclined. I am speaking here of the temptation to overestimate one's powers.

It is certainly not those who are weakest in their striving to reach the Spirit's Light who are most at risk of overestimating their powers.

Because of their exaggerated confidence, these enthusiasts believe themselves able to advance on their path in leaps and bounds, and imagine that they can achieve in months what others need years, or even a lifetime, to master.

When the mind is overcome by a burning sense of urgency to experience the bliss of the Eternal, it creates a constant state of anxiety in the impatient seeker, which may in turn cause serious psychological and physical damage. But one can never reach the goal when it is sought for in such a desperate and tormented manner.

Such seekers rack their brains relentlessly and cause themselves needless torment. But the path that leads one to the Spirit requires the very opposite: a mind that can be both awake and still, an inner calm and patience to await one's progress towards the goal.

Impatience and incessant longing not only lead seekers astray but also, as is the case with ascetics, put them in danger of being deceived.

To be sure, it has been written that only through the use of violence can one draw close to "the kingdom of heaven."* But one can only understand what is meant here by "violence" if one considers the words spoken by Jacob as he wrestled with the angel: "I will not let thee go, except thou bless me." (Genesis 32:26 King James Version)

What is meant here by "violence" is not the intention to overpower another but, rather, a tenacious holding fast to something greatly valued, even while one is aware of one's own weakness, powerlessness and smallness.

Those who are so attached to this word that they cannot let go of it are advised to direct the "violence" they think they cannot do without towards subduing those thoughts in their restless, brooding minds that do nothing but create obstacles that stand in the way of reaching the goal.

---

*". . . the kingdom of heaven suffereth violence, and the violent take it by force." (Matthew 11:12) This is considered to be one of the most controversial passages in the Bible, and has been the subject of much scholarly commentary.

Those of my pupils who have entered onto the path to the goal I have shown them, and who pursue it in a manner suited to their own nature, must never rush or force their way, or try to track it down as a hunter might his prey.

With sure confidence and patient perseverance, they must carefully take one step after another, always remaining true to the way they have selected from my texts that is most in accord with their individual nature. This path is not to be abandoned even once the goal is reached, for it then becomes the seeker's cherished, eternal possession.

Those who have reached the goal will have need of this path—which has opened to them through their own efforts—so that the consciousness of the eternal Spirit that is now theirs will remain united with their timeless soul. It is the timeless soul that allows this consciousness to partake of our life on earth, and to gather memories of our mortal identity. The soul carries these memories into the realm of Eternity, and thus guarantees that our individual identity will be preserved in our spiritual existence after death.

The path into the Spirit is traversed in earthly time but within one's inner, spiritual space.

In just the same way, the goal is reached in earthly time and yet is only found in spiritual, internal space.

Therefore, it is of no use to search for the way in the outer world, mistakenly believing that the goal may more readily be reached in one place than another.

The image of a path one walks on as earthly time passes has been intentionally chosen as a metaphor for progress on the inner journey.

It is no coincidence that this metaphor has been used since ancient times by those whose teaching is rooted in the Spirit.

Even though the goal is found within one's own inner, spiritual space, seekers may yet need to travel infinite distances to reach it.

They must journey through the world of earthly time which day by day will bring them ever closer to fulfillment.

As they awaken, they will travel through ever deeper levels of awareness that follow one upon another, each of which can be distinctly felt.

Each level arises from the one preceding it and is dependent on it having been consciously attained, and none may be skipped over or thought to be unneeded.

※

Seekers torment themselves needlessly when they worry that their progress is too slow or feel anxious because they are impatient to reach the end of their path, yet realize that they are only at its start.

It is only beneficial to know where one stands because, otherwise, seekers may become overconfident and fool themselves into believing they have walked further on the path than is true, only to later face bitter disappointment.

Some of those who consider themselves to be my pupils, simply because they are "familiar" with everything I have written, exacerbate their needless self-torment when they try to speed up the natural pace of their progress by delving into questionable philosophies or occult literature. Such sources may use the same terms as I do, but they have little to do with my teachings, both with regard to the way the path is to be pursued and the nature of the ultimate goal.

THE PATH OF MY PUPILS

I might smile at these attempts to "help things along" in the way one smiles at the follies of small children, not yet old enough to know better, were it not for the fact that I have witnessed, again and again, how seekers obstruct their own path by looking elsewhere to find what they *think* is missing from my writings.

For this reason, with the seekers own best interest in mind, I must refuse to accept any responsibility for the results of such foolhardy comingling of teachings that are in essence incompatible and which can only lead to self-deception.

ALL WHO BELIEVE they can advance more easily on their own instead of diligently adhering to the instructions given by me in full awareness of my responsibility to the Eternal realm are well advised to leave my books unread so that, at very least, they will not be guilty of misusing them.

Those who consider themselves to be my pupils, even though they make mention of my teachings in the same breath as they do a plethora of irresponsible rubbish and other bits of "wisdom" should draw a lesson from the fact that, among those pupils who I acknowledge to be mine, and who are most advanced, there is not a single one who does not focus with strictest self-discipline on the instructions I have given—and only on them—in pursuit of the goal.

This is by no means surprising, since the teachings I have clad in the garment of words have been tried and tested for thousands of years—just as I have given them.

To believe that one can achieve more than is possible through following the guidance given in my books by simultaneously following all kinds of other human opinions and ideas is completely contrary to the requirements for progress on the path that leads to the eternal Spirit.

CHAPTER FOUR

UNAVOIDABLE DIFFICULTIES

WHENEVER HUMAN BEINGS ATTEMPT TO communicate experiences arising from regions not accessible to most others on earth, they face the difficult challenge of how to convey what is in essence inexpressible in words, and the limitations of the listeners' capacity to understand what has been communicated.

Such difficulties are further complicated when the experiences being reported are very different from anything that is familiar to most people, so that comparisons to everyday experience are impossible to find, and one can only bring about a kind of understanding through imagery, metaphor, and allusion.

All these problems exist, most assuredly, with regard to what I have come to say.

❦

THE PATH OF MY PUPILS

M*y obligation* and task would be far easier if my teachings were intended only for the peoples of Asia, for whom many of the concepts I convey have been alive for thousand of years—and indeed may be part of their inborn heritage. By no means, however, would all difficulties be removed.

One set of problems would merely be exchanged for another in that those who misinterpret my words would find justification for their views in various religious and philosophical systems.

Those who I am obliged to call my spiritual "brothers"—all of whom live in Asia, although they are not all of the same ethnic group—are fully aware of such difficulties and understand that any attempt to convey these same teachings to their own peoples would be too great a sacrifice, for it would not bear a corresponding reward.

They even believe that it would be far more possible for my teachings to reach the regions in which they currently live, and to attract an ever-widening circle of souls mature enough to receive them, if transmitted from Europe. It would be more difficult for Asians to maintain the integrity of these teachings and guard them from the influence of local religious beliefs—from the errors and grotesque interpretations and a superstitious hunger for miracles that would follow were they to say the same things I say in my books.

Given that such obstacles are present in these vast regions of the earth, where countless human beings have, through their age-old heritage of wisdom and tradition of spiritual discipleship, attained knowledge I try to make comprehensible to Westerners, how much more surely will my teachings encounter serious barriers to understanding, albeit of a different kind, in the Western world.

I do not, however, consider these problems to be insurmountable, although I must confess that I would be no less obligated to carry out my task were I to have doubts about my being equal to its challenges, or feel pessimistic about the impact of my teaching.

If i were not who I in fact am—through no choice of my own—I too would have great difficulties were I to come across the teachings that bear my name, without prior preparation and tied to preconceived, traditional religious and philosophical ways of thinking.

Let no one think that I cannot understand how problematic it must be for Westerners today—inflated with smug certainty about the causes of all phenomena—to take seriously what I have to tell them.

I myself am, after all, a human being of this time of transition, familiar with its intellectual achievements and its methods of scientific thought, aware of its genuine accomplishments as well as its over-confident ambitions. Also, I cannot deny that because of the spiritual organs of perception that are active in me, I am aware of connections and can penetrate the nature of phenomena that most others cannot perceive, even those who are certain that nothing escapes their finely-honed sensibilities.

I am only too well aware of the obstacles that minds shaped by European or American thinking must overcome if they are to grasp what is offered in my books—teachings offered by me but truly not conceived by me.

These are teachings that exist and have existed for all time within the realm of the Eternal and which have been accessible to all who are of my kind since the beginnings of human life on this planet.

The fact that there have always been very few of my kind is required by spiritual law.

THE HUMAN cranium is by no means a hermetic seal and so does not isolate the brain completely from external vibrations. Similarly, the forces from which the soul forms itself organically can never be completely isolated from contact with the all-conscious, all-feeling, and all-knowing within the vast and immeasurable sea of free and unbounded soul forces.

Human beings are in fact familiar with far more than they are consciously aware of, although what is familiar may first need to be called forth—by a word, a visible object, or an inner experience—in order to become conscious.

Souls that are not crippled are already more familiar with what I have to offer than those for whom the mind is their only source of light—a light that flickers restlessly and is impermanent.

In order to avoid any misunderstandings, I must emphasize that the terms "unconscious," and "collective unconscious," as popularized by psychoanalysis and its offshoots, in no way correspond to what I am trying to convey.

We are not dealing here with something once accessible to the conscious mind which has since been lost but, rather, with something familiar to the eternal soul, which has not yet become perceptible to the conscious mind.

My pupils can best avoid misinterpreting my words if they absorb my way of expressing those things I have myself experienced with openness and free of preconceptions, and avoid completely the attempt to fit what I convey into scholarly and scientific concepts that are ever-changing.

I could certainly make use of such concepts but I am more comfortable when I allow myself the freedom to choose the words that feel most useful to me in conveying the meaning I intend, without concern for their conventional use.

Many an obstacle to understanding is already cleared away if one realizes that I speak above all to the soul, relying on the familiarity of the soul with matters not yet accessible to the mind.

If readers of my books can manage, at least for a moment and to some degree, to resist the loud, intrusive clamor and the false assurance of the intellect, so that whatever is familiar to the soul, yet still not comprehended by the mind, can be called up to their consciousness, they will have opened within themselves the gateway of the path to the Spirit—the path that my teachings guide them to follow.

Readers who have attained this inner state will encounter few major difficulties, provided they possess the perseverance that is essential for all who wish to journey on the path that leads into the Spirit.

To be sure, what I have to convey must be taken on faith until such time as pupils arrive at the insights that will enable them to judge for themselves.

THE PATH OF MY PUPILS

Those who search for guidance will have to find their own way of absorbing what I offer them in my teachings, and would be well advised not to mingle it with other teachings, no matter what their source.

Pupils who wish to arrive at their own insights should, for the time being, set aside even those teachings which stem, without the slightest doubt, from the most sincere and venerable of individuals—if they would benefit from my guidance.

Only when seekers have achieved all that is possible within themselves can they fully understand the wisdom of the teachings to be found in Medieval and—with a different coloration—Eastern mysticism.

At the same time, they will be able to recognize the many errors that have inadvertently crept in among these testimonies of Truth, imparted by human beings close to or even united with the Spirit. They will not hesitate to separate the "chaff" from the living seed of "wheat," even though this chaff is far more abundant than they might have thought.

Until they have progressed this far, however, they will do well to forget all they know of such teachings.

It goes without saying that the formulas for spiritual development propounded by modern mystagogues, which seekers may have followed up until now, will have to be put aside for good.

Even if I now, out of respect for what is conveyed through my writings, must ask for a certain degree of trust until such time as a pupil's own ability to judge has matured, I do not ask for "belief" in the sense of a final commitment. I ask, rather, for the kind of trust one would place in the captain of a ship who knows how to navigate the high seas and bring its passengers to safe harbor, or a conscientious mountain guide who knows that the lives of those entrusted to his care depend on his judgment and sure knowledge of the paths.

Just as one gives mountain guides the right to advise on how best to climb among the rocks, or how to traverse difficult glacier crossings, in the same way, pupils should accept the counsel they find in my books.

I know the dangers they will meet on their path and I am able to advise them how to overcome those dangers.

Nothing could be further from my intention than to demand blind, slavish obedience. I would not claim the right to demand such a thing, nor do I regard it as being in the best interest of my pupils or in any way desirable.

Pupils should be given enough information to know, or to at least be able to form an idea of what they may expect on their path and why I impart certain advice or warn of particular dangers.

Much of what I have written in my books was unspeakably difficult for me to set down on paper, because I was forced to describe in ordinary words that which I have suffered, experienced and received—things that are indescribably high and so far beyond all that may be suffered, experienced and received here on earth that only after the most solemn preparation do I dare even recall them to memory.

I could have saved myself the grueling ordeal that has gone into producing each sentence if I could have fulfilled my spiritual duty to give those who search for guidance a multidimensional, living insight into the nature of events in the realm of Spirit in some other way.

Everything in my books has been given to my readers for the sole purpose of insuring that they do not follow my advice out of blind and unquestioning trust. Rather, once they have been able to comprehend, or at least conceptualize, the spiritual relationships on which my advice is based, they should be free to use their own judgment and to consult their own conscience in adapting my advice in the way that is most suitable to them.

I must insist, however, that my pupils rely solely on my written words as the basis for their decisions—and disregard my person.

Those who would be my pupils should know that I have given myself to them in my writing without reservation and that they are only "my" pupils to the degree that they are able to learn from and apply my texts. The absolute Truth of these texts as a depiction of real and tangible spiritual reality cannot be shaken even if they had not been written by someone with a deep and profound sense of responsibility to the eternal Spirit and in complete possession of his mental faculties but, rather—were such a thing even possible—by a fool.

When I use the term "tangible spiritual reality" I ask my readers to bear in mind that I am referring to the true and ultimate Reality, the profuse, primordial energies of Being—in contrast to reality as perceived by the rational mind and mental activity.

This tangible, spiritual "substance" is not at all rigid or fixed in form but, rather, in its very nature completely free and unobstructed, eternally changing and forever in motion.

It is not, as some might suppose, "created" by a special act of will but is instead perpetually in existence, by virtue of the energies of "primordial Being"—the name I use to designate the innermost of all that is.

Even the most subtle energies of the universe, whose existence today's most brilliant physicists have only just begun to suspect, are only a kind of "effect" caused by the spiritual substance to which I have referred—analogous to the way electrical current can be indirectly induced in a secondary coil by a primary induction coil, and transformed into a different frequency. Less refined energies, such as those known to us as electricity and magnetism, are only the reflexive results, so to speak, of that "induction effect."

It is impossible for me to be any clearer here, but I have good reason to believe that future scientific research will yield insights, verifiable by physical phenomena, that will open up an entirely new and comprehensive field of investigation, which I have only touched on here.

A TRUE AWAKENING to the nature of the radiant, eternal Spirit is beyond all science. Even the loftiest scientific insights cannot bring one a hair's breadth closer to the majesty of personal experience within the Spirit's realm.

It should be understood, therefore, that once those who seek the Spirit begin their journey on the path, although filled almost to excess with my teachings, they will need help from a source other than myself, the one who prepares and instructs them on the path.

This kind of help is always at hand and seekers may call upon it readily by simply cultivating an attitude of inner confidence and grateful expectation.

No "god" can offer this help. Only a fellow human being can bring direct assistance and thus, divine help can only be transmitted to us through a human being who has become a transformer of the Spirit's radiant energies.

The spiritual help that reaches human beings is always in proportion to their ability to receive it and remains this way until such time as they awaken in their innermost, and thus are able to experience the radiant eternal Spirit within their own spiritual organism. This is so whether the process necessary to reach this state can be completed during the person's life on earth or, as is usually the case, is only begun here and is completed in stages of existence after death.

In the path towards the awakening of the soul, there are innumerable stages of unfolding and so it is with the only true experience of God

UNAVOIDABLE DIFFICULTIES

that human beings can have access to—the experience of the Living God within one's soul.

⁕

"G<small>OD</small>" IS NOT ONLY Spirit but, more precisely, the Spirit forming itself, out of its own substance, refined to highest purity. The experience of God does not require the spiritual organism to have attained perfection; it is enough that this organism has been awakened and so is able to light up that distinctive consciousness of the timeless self within the soul. It is this unique form of consciousness that alone makes possible the experience of the eternal.

Those human beings who have had this experience will no longer ask if, indeed, it has truly happened or wonder if they have merely succumbed to a form of self-deception—because what they now experience illuminates the inner Being with the most profound, unshakable certainty that may be found on earth or in the realm of Eternity.

Those who still find themselves questioning whether their sublime experience was indeed real—even if only in those dark hours that come, unavoidably, to everyone—may assume that they in some way influenced their own experience and then convinced themselves of its authenticity. The sooner seekers free themselves from such self-deception the sooner will they be able to attain a true experience of their Living God within.

True experience of the Divine will never overwhelm the soul. It always molds itself to fit the nature of the person so that they are never forced to stretch beyond their tolerance.

This is why I say in my teachings that it is only possible to experience one's own Living God and none shall ever, here on earth and in all eternity, be able to show their Living God to another.

Any attempt to "make" such an experience happen will lead to self-deception.

The word "grace," although greatly misused and, therefore, almost never used by me, is nonetheless appropriate here as it conveys the essence of this experience—provided one understands that this word is being used to mean the receipt of a blessing for which one has fulfilled all the prerequisites, so that this blessing must be granted because it cannot be withheld, not even by divine will.

Whether an individual has had this experience only once or repeatedly, or it is for them an ongoing state of being, depends on what is possible for that particular soul. But all who have had it, in whatever manner is suitable for them, enter a new life and experience a renewal which can only be felt but can never be expressed in words.

CHAPTER FIVE

DYNAMIC FAITH

It is a truism that any human endeavor will only be successful if those who embark on it believe that it is possible and feel confident they can reach the goal.

Most people have learned this truth through personal experience; those who have not, will not have far to look to find individuals whose successes or failures serve as examples of it.

Individuals with great talent, who have every reason to have high hopes for success, often fail to reach their goal, simply because they lack faith in their abilities, while others with only mediocre talents go from success to success, because they believe so firmly in themselves.

And how often have we heard of inspired individuals who failed to bring their vision to fruition, even after a lifetime of exhausting effort, only to have those who follow in their footsteps succeed where they did not. This because those followers were imbued with greater confidence and faith in their ultimate success, even though they might have been possessed of lesser talent.

On any street corner one can encounter individuals from all walks of life who, with best of intentions, try tenaciously to reach some goal, while at the same time lacking the belief that they will ever reach it.

Is it any wonder then that so few reach that goal to which I show the path in all my books. And yet it can be reached by all who are imbued with faith—faith in themselves.

This is the meaning of the saying "God helps those who help themselves."

This saying does not call into question the truth that divine help is always at hand but, rather, tells us what we must do *ourselves* in order to prepare the way for it to come to us.

Belief in God is only self-deception if it does not rest on the solid bedrock of belief in one's own self.

DYNAMIC FAITH

Belief is will—and those who do not know their belief to be a form of will, know nothing of belief.

One should be careful, though, to distinguish between true will and wishes that are obstinately and tenaciously clung to.

We commonly speak of "will" in situations where, in fact, it is only the wild and unrealistic wish that is striving towards the goal—while the will that has the power to attain that goal lies fast asleep.

But when we say that "faith is will" then we must also say that the will that is demanded here is nothing other than the power of imagination. Through this majestic power human beings shape their destiny, both in the outer world and in striving towards their highest goal within the world of Spirit.

WHERE IT CONCERNS the healing of the body's ailments, these principles are common knowledge. Thus, wise physicians seek to awaken their patients' "will to recovery" and liberate its power from the shackles their patients' disbelief has forged around it.

The "miraculous" cures that once brought fame to the temple of Asclepius at Epidaurus or the cures for which the faithful flock to Lourdes today, both owe their miracle-working power to the stimulation of the will to recover, the freeing of the imagination, and a belief in the possibility of health regained—even if these merely fulfill the requirements that must be met to pave the way for helping forces of a different kind.

※

THROUGHOUT THE ages tales have been told of sacred places where the sick were healed, and also tales of individuals who had the power to heal where medicines and potions could do nothing. The miraculous cures attributed to these healers are due to nothing other than their ability to awaken in their patients faith in the ability to heal and the intention to recover—the all-important "will" to recovery—so that the mental image of sickness they have harbored is replaced with one of health regained.

To be sure, not every illness can be healed in this way. Fervent believers are all too willing to overlook the fact that many sufferers have come away from places of pilgrimage still unhealed, or only seemingly healed, and often healers too have been unable to cure them.

However, only a fool would deny that faith has the power to affect the physical body in most extraordinary ways.

THE EFFECT a living faith has on the physical body is great indeed, but greater still is the power a clearly focused faith can have to shape the spiritual body—the invisible organism of the Spirit.

Those whose physical illness is of the type that can be cured through faith must summon the power of imagination to visualize themselves as healthy, in the same way they previously used that power to see themselves as ill. Just so, those who wish to reach their highest goal within the Spirit's realm must harness the power of faith to imagine within themselves the spiritual form into which they wish to be transformed.

Even the most ardent wish has never been able to transform one who is seeking into one who has found the sought-for goal within the Spirit's realm.

One must have certain *faith* that one will find that which one is seeking before the sublime goal can be reached.

The only kind of faith that leads to the divine is the belief in oneself, and only this creative will can inspire within the seekers' soul a vision of the being they need become.

Once this inner image is clear within the mind, the seekers' invisible, spiritual organism will pattern itself after this image and will become transformed in such a way that seekers will be ever more able to find that which they desire.

M‍ost people believe that the ability to penetrate the sacred realm of Spirit is beyond their reach, the exclusive province of a chosen few that they themselves, by their very nature, cannot enter. They have been misled by false teachings and have lost faith in their own divine nature. True guidance and sure faith is needed to restore them to the knowledge that it is their calling—the calling of each human being—to unite with God.

Trust and inner certainty that the highest goal can truly be attained must first and foremost come alive in those who would approach the realm of living, radiant Spirit and all that awaits them there.

Timidity must be conquered and self-doubt overcome. No one can approach the eternal realm through "fear and trembling" despite the fact that these misguided words, so very far from truth, have been given credence here on earth for millennia.

Countless are those who have spent a lifetime searching but never finding what they sought, because they heeded this false guidance and quashed their inner confidence.

Without the faith of which I speak no mortal may gain entrance to the realm of radiant Spirit. This faith can only become a living and dynamic force if those who search have unshakable inner confidence and know that they indeed can reach their highest goal.

So long as seekers lack this living and dynamic inner confidence, all high help that is continuously offered to human beings as they turn from the darkness of this material world towards the path to light is rendered powerless.

Only those who absolutely trust themselves are able to trust also in the help that is offered to them from on high—the help they cannot do without as they ascend the steep path to the radiant Spirit.

Only those who absolutely trust themselves are able to call forth a living and dynamic faith within—and only this faith can transform the *wish* to reach salvation into the *will* that can achieve it.

※

All my teachings have at their foundation the understanding that one must say a resounding "yes" to oneself, regardless of all one's faults and failings—which must of course, also be acknowledged.

In my books I clearly state that human beings must first understand, in the depths of their being, that they *originate* from the realm of the eternal Spirit, before they can hope to return to their home in the Spirit once more.

Even with the best of intentions, it is not possible for those who seek the Spirit to make use of the teachings I offer so long as they lack an unwavering belief in themselves and in the truth of their eternal, spiritual nature.

This belief cannot simply be a mere assumption or a matter of supposing something to be true.

Only a dynamic faith—the faith that is a living energy and which generates more energy from within itself—can impart the inner certainty that must fill the heart of everyone who would tread the path that leads into the Spirit.

In contrast, a "belief" in the mental image of what one desires to become, without dynamic faith, is more a hindrance than a help, no matter whether this image is an accurate reflection of what is possible or not.

I do not describe the worlds that cannot be seen by the physical eye in order to create mental pictures in the minds of my pupils but, rather, to build a bridge of understanding so that those who seek may know why I am obliged, in their own interest, to make the demands I do on their will to pursue the inner path.

Wherever it seems to the reader that there are contradictions in these descriptions, I advise my readers to let the matter rest, until such time as their faith clears the way for understanding, so that apparent contradictions are resolved.

A living, dynamic faith is secure and strong enough to remain unshaken even if one misunderstands my descriptions of states of being that truly cannot be described in words.

CHAPTER SIX

THE GREATEST OBSTACLE

THE GREATEST OBSTACLE ON THE INNER PATH for those who aspire to find the Spirit is not a precipitous skepticism too quickly ready to doubt but, rather, a paralyzing fear that hides behind many different masks.

Even skepticism is in most cases *fear* cloaked in a compulsive need to question each and every thing.

Fear of making a mistake or, worse yet, fear of having to revise one's own world view, and fear of being ridiculed by others.

Human beings like to give each other logical and high-minded reasons for their actions while their motivation is, in truth, some form of fear that lies hidden underneath.

Or they hide from fear behind an empty screen of words so they do not have to see its face.

There are more victims of fear in the world than ever were brought down by deadly plagues.

Is it any wonder then that those who seek their timeless selves, and the living God enthroned in royal glory and concealed within them, are beset by fears as well. They too must often struggle with resistance to their progress that originates within themselves.

It is surely not easy to conquer one's fears, but it is more difficult to uncover them when they are veiled and disguised beneath many masks, and easier to face them once their source is understood.

Those who would make progress on the path should carefully examine what they believe to be the reasons, motives, or intentions behind their actions, so as to unearth the fears that may lie buried underneath.

If they overlook even one such hidden fear, then it will be as if the enemy has taken up residence in their home—and because they

THE GREATEST OBSTACLE

failed to recognize its presence, they will be unable to evict it.

Fear has been responsible for more folly and senseless cruelty in the world than those beset by it suspect or are willing to admit.

Wherever one looks, one sees countless instances in which fear is the true motivation that lies behind people's decisions.

Fear of this, that and the other—fear of a multitude of things, concealed behind the most elusive of masks.

Fear may torment those who journey on the inner path in the guise of a "guilty conscience." They cannot comprehend that the realm of the eternal Spirit remains always open to them, despite all their missteps and shortcomings.

However, the pangs of anxiety that arise from a guilty conscience are not always a true reflection of reality.

Those who are burdened by a guilty conscience may simply have allowed too much to weigh on their conscience; whereas, a person of conscience would not have allowed themselves to be so burdened.

※

I<small>N TIMES OF</small> distress, pupils would do well to pay no attention to their inner progress and to avoid the tendency to be preoccupied with themselves, until such time as they are able to overcome their fears and anxieties, be those fears apparent or disguised.

They will lose nothing by doing so, for nothing good can ever come forth from fear.

Once the fear has dissipated, no matter what manner of fear or anxiety it was, they will discover that their progress on the inner path was not at all halted during their self-imposed pause.

Fear and anxiety can only persist when one doubts one's worthiness to reach the inner goal. When one is beset by self-doubt one should refrain from working on one's inner self.

※

O<small>NE CAN SEARCH</small> the world in vain to find a positive deed done under the hypnotic spell of fear.

THE GREATEST OBSTACLE

Whenever people claim that something good has come from fear, we can be sure that they have misinterpreted what has actually transpired. They have failed to notice that the good did not in fact result from fear but, rather, from that moment "in between" when the clouds of fear were parted and before they closed in once again—a brief reprieve or clearing that allowed the good to enter.

Constant fear is worse than sudden fright because it dams up every crevice through which courage might yet flow into one's being; whereas, in moments of sudden fright, it is as if courage is temporarily "forgotten," only to be "remembered" with renewed strength once the initial shock has passed.

Constant fear and anxiety, however, block courage completely.

Those who are gripped by anxiety and fear may regard the exhortation to simply lay aside their fears and overcome their loss of courage as an unwelcome intrusion into their autonomy.

Fear may be likened to a state of self-hypnosis. If at the moment that the clouds of fear have lifted, one makes the determination to master the spell of fear should it descend again, one may then free oneself more quickly.

Those susceptible to anxiety and fear cannot give themselves such a command often enough.

If pupils on the path to the Spirit allow states of fear to live within them, they run the risk of compromising the success of all their inner progress.

They must tell themselves again and again that there is absolutely nothing to fear.

As long as their own will is aligned with their spiritual striving, and does not stand in opposition to it, they will be aided in their efforts to ward off anxiety and fear. Sublime helpers will be at their side, giving them added power and inner fortitude.

Once seekers have freed themselves from fear, they will discover again and again that all of their anxieties were caused by phantoms of their own making.

Many people have died an unintended death because their life energies were shattered by these imaginary threats.

THE GREATEST OBSTACLE

Death from sheer, consuming fear is not as rare an occurrence as one might think.

❧

F<small>EAR LIVES ONLY</small> *within* the human being; it has no existence in the outer world.

Fear does not exist within the world of Spirit; therefore, one cannot experience fear within one's soul, even though people may speak of a fear that grips them to their depths.

All forms of anxiety and fear, whether they are apparent or masked, are nothing more than a kind of "cramping" of certain delicate nerves. Such cramping occurs when disturbing mental images or thoughts affect the brain. Thus, it is a reaction that takes place solely in the physical realm, because the brain and its consciousness are part of the physical body.

The mental images and thoughts that may give rise to this type of cramp, which is perceived as anxiety or fear, may relate to the realm of Spirit or the soul, as well as the physical world. One should not be misled, however, into assuming that such fear originates from, or exists within, the realm of Spirit or the soul.

❧

Fear can only be overcome if the images and thoughts that give rise to it are clearly recognized and the fear-inducing elements within these images and thoughts are dissolved through a process of detached and sober observation.

These thoughts and mental images vary among fear-prone individuals, and the same individual may suffer from different fears at different times; therefore, one should give oneself the mental command referred to above repeatedly and often, so as to immediately interrupt the fear-cramp and "awaken" from its spell.

Thereafter, it is essential to isolate in one's mind the fear-provoking images and thoughts and dispassionately examine them.

Once these elements have been accurately identified they may be easily dissolved and drained of their power.

❧

THE GREATEST OBSTACLE

It is not my intention to discuss matters that are the province of the medical profession, but simply to provide my pupils with instructions as to how they may clear the greatest obstacle to progress on their inner path.

Such instructions are especially needed because even those who show the most courage in their outer life succumb at times to the most curious—and disguised—states of fear once they have begun to work seriously on the development of their spiritual organism.

This fear is understandable because the spiritual organism, which is composed of spiritual substance, is largely unknown to the mortal human creature, and whatever is unknown seems strange and unnatural to the purely physical consciousness of the mind. Many people train their physical bodies in order to achieve a level of peak performance; others do the same with their minds, while others still cultivate their emotional life. But most people are unaware of their spiritual organism; it is experienced as a foreign region and is therefore instinctively avoided and so remains in a state of latency.

The unknown and unexplored is the ideal breeding ground for every fear-born, dreadful fantasy that the human imagination can produce.

As long as such disquieting images—images that have their origin in remnants of fairy tales heard in early childhood that have settled in the brain like sediment, in religious pronouncements once believed in, and in memories of real or imaginary "guilt"—are not banished once and for all, a resolute pursuit of the inner path that leads into the Spirit will remain almost impossible.

For this reason, seekers have the obligation to examine the real motives behind their thoughts, words, and deeds on a daily basis, so as to gradually become able to recognize fear in all its disguises and drive it out from its hiding places.

This way of monitoring one's inner life is far more beneficial than constantly "examining one's conscience" in search of every little shred of real or imagined "guilt"—a curse which those with conscientious natures fall victim to most easily.

CHAPTER SEVEN

PUPILS AND THEIR COMPANIONS

Nothing could be more detrimental on the path to the Spirit that the true pupil walks upon than a competitive spirit.

In other human endeavors, the eagerness to know more and be capable of greater accomplishment than others can help to advance the person so motivated. In the spiritual realm, however, the slightest wish to outdo one's fellow seekers on the path will only serve to retard one's progress.

But stirrings of envy that are not instantly mastered and permanently extinguished will cause greater harm still. Envy will bring all spiritual growth to a complete halt, no matter what further efforts the pupil might make.

Only when pupils have eradicated the very last trace of envy that stirs within them, may they hope to make further progress on the path.

※

In these matters there can be no "exceptions"; no special status for particular individuals, no matter how prestigious their place in society or even if they have made contributions to humanity for which all are indebted.

This is the law of the Spirit; the inexorable law that emanates from the Spirit's life and is inherent within it and inseparable from it—and can never be transgressed.

Nothing can ever take place within the realm of the Spirit that does not align itself with the Spirit's law—not even the most insignificant event, not even that which might occur at the outer limits of that realm.

The Spirit's law concerns only the spiritual dimension within the human being.

While it matters greatly to the inner life of human beings on this earth that they awaken to the Spirit, such consciousness is of no concern to Spirit; the Spirit remains forever part of every individual, whether or not they are conscious of its abiding presence.

One must not be led astray by sentimental dreams of a deity that experiences human suffering as its own and awaits redemption by humanity. Such fantastic notions are very far from reality and may, at best, be allowed to poets.

Reality is quite different from this.

Pupils should always bear in mind what I attempt to communicate about the nature of the Ground of all Being, the primordial foundation that is common to all life. Even though I feel the inadequacy of trying to convey my meaning more painfully here than in any other matters—I must accept this pain.

My books convey matters that are beyond description and sublime; yet, there exists within every human being a natural urge to create mental pictures of all things, and this impulse must be tempered by guidance.

I speak with deepest reverence of a most sublime trinity to which I give the names Primordial Being, Primordial Light and Primordial Word, whose essence I attempt to make understandable in human language—with trembling adoration—by referring to the three aspects in which they are expressed: the Primordial Human of the Spirit, Primordial Light and Primordial Word. I endeavor to show how this Primordial Human of the Spirit is both "Father" and "Mother" to the human being, and the human being is itself a trinity comprised of spirit, soul and mind.

I endeavor to show how, through this pathway, the true human is able to touch the very heights of the Spirit and reach upward to the innermost of the Godhead itself, which lovingly unites with each human being and manifests as their own Living God.

Finally, it is my task to explain that what we refer to as the "human being" here on earth is not the human being of Eternity but, rather, the earthbound creature in which the eternal human spirit seeks to experience itself. This state has come about because emanations of eternal Spirit strove to go beyond what was meant to be their highest state of being in the realm of Spirit—thus making it inevitable that they should "fall." Such a fall is "sinful" for this striving violates the innate order of the Spirit's realm. There is no way for such fallen spirits to redeem themselves and regain what they have lost other than to become incarnate in one of the innocent, physical creatures of the universe—an animal. And the only animal form that can be of use here is one that by its nature can become an expression of the eternal human being.

This is the animal form we know only too well from our own physical experience.

As familiar as we are, with this animal form—which we call "the human animal"—as well acquainted as we are with its needs, inclinations and drives, we are nonetheless equally ready to deny the reality of many of its attributes. We find it difficult to admit that we have more in common with other animals than we would like to think. The one trait, however that we cannot claim to share with other animals is their innocence. For human beings, such a state of pure, animal-like innocence is the province of childhood alone and could we, as adults, experience just one moment of such pure innocence again, we would long to return to it forever.

Not only do we like to consider our faculties of reasoning to be unique to ourselves, and not shared with other animals—like nouveau riches who try to obscure their origins—we are even inclined to deny that our fellow animals possess what we commonly refer to as a "soul." The mortal "soul" of humans rises above the primitive level of other animals and becomes more developed in human beings only when it is intentionally refined through our own efforts.

Pupils should keep in mind that nearly everything we commonly refer to as emanating from the "soul" actually pertains to the perishable soul of our animal nature—a soul that endures only so long as we remain alive on earth. We share this type of soul with other animals but it attains in us a greater richness of emotion and expression due to the influence of our *imperishable*, eternal soul, which emanates from the energies of the Godhead and is unique to human beings.

This distinction will help avoid misunderstanding that may impede the pupil's spiritual development.

Overweening ambition for spiritual accomplishment, competitiveness and envy, all of which can severely impede our spiritual development, originate in our perishable, animal soul.

IT GOES WITHOUT saying that pupils should try, insofar as possible, to subordinate the energies of their perishable, animal soul to the energies of their eternal soul—the soul forces that are uniquely theirs as human beings and emanate from out of the Godhead.

Thus, all impulses of the animal soul that are in harmony with the goal of unifying the energies of the eternal soul forces within one's eternal "I"—that constellation of elements that together form our own eternal being and through which we experience all things in the Spirit's realm—must be nourished, cared for and enlisted in the service of this sacred task.

All impulses of the animal soul that are not in harmony with the goal—impulses that might hinder the unification of the eternal soul forces within the eternal "I" or the unfolding of the timeless human being's spiritual organism—

must be allowed to gradually subside, just as a musical note slowly fades away when no further energy is added to it. And even if this process, like all transformative processes, takes time and cannot be rushed, it is nonetheless essential to resist energizing these impulses by action or thought, right from the very start.

The desire to outpace one's fellow pupils on the path, as well as feelings of envy about their level of spiritual development, are merely manifestations of the animal soul and can be compared to the competition and envy for food that we so commonly observe among animals.

Those who seek to progress on the inner path must not only learn to master these lower impulses that derive from their animal soul; they must also strive to awaken the opposite feelings within their eternal soul.

They must not rest until they are able to be filled with joy when learning that one of their fellow pupil's spiritual development has exceeded their own.

And they must consider it their duty to offer all possible assistance to fellow pupils who have fallen behind.

Those human beings who are called "masters" of the art of living in the three worlds—the world of reason and mental comprehension, the world of the soul forces, and the world of the radiant, eternal Spirit—would never act otherwise.

They see some of their "brothers" traversing almost unattainable heights and others still wandering through lowlands they themselves have long ago left behind or never even had to pass through.

If I or one of my brothers could look up to the heights and see an exalted brother, without feeling intense joy, or look down to the depths and see a struggling brother, without feeling a burning desire to help—then we would have ceased being what we are and would no longer be able to act as Mediators of eternal Light.

Another impulse of the animal soul that pupils on the path must learn to overcome right from the start is the malicious urge to discover the faults and shortcomings of fellow seekers—and perhaps to even point these out to others.

This impulse, too, is a fatal obstacle to true spiritual development and until the very last trace of it has been eliminated all supposed progress on the path amounts to nothing more than self-deception.

Pupils who expect guidance and support from the radiant, eternal Spirit should not even wish to see the faults and errors of their companions and if they unavoidably do become aware of such shortcomings, it is their duty to ignore them.

However, if such shortcomings could lead to significant harm for the person concerned, or to others, so that they cannot in good conscience be ignored, then the one who has involuntarily discovered these defects should inform those—and only those—who can be trusted to have no other concern than to protect the person and others from harm.

PUPILS AND THEIR COMPANIONS

Here, too, one may draw a parallel with the Luminaries—those beings who mediate eternal Light.

Because the time of a Luminary's physical incarnation is determined thousands of years in advance, and given that at such time he must be born into a physical body that will have all the psycho-physical traits required for the task accorded to him, it often cannot be avoided that this body will also have certain other traits that are unwanted. The Luminary may be barely able to keep such traits in check because his energies are required elsewhere. Were he to struggle with such tendencies and try to truly subdue them—as desirable as that might be—he would impair the psycho-physical energies needed for his work to an irresponsible degree.

These problematic weaknesses that are a part of a Luminary's mortal, physical nature can include every sort of inclination that the physical body might be prone to. They may manifest to a certain degree in any area of earthly endeavor even though he will constantly erect new barriers that will prevent the most extreme expressions of such undesirable tendencies.

No Mediator of eternal Light has ever harbored the childish, foolish conceit of wanting to be regarded as a "Saint" —nor could such a thing even be possible for someone who has attained this level of inner development.

Woe to the Luminary—no matter how exalted his position within the Spirit's realm— who is incapable of meeting a spiritual brother's earthly shortcomings with anything other than humor and understanding.

When I speak of a Luminary who feels superior to a spiritual brother who has erred in earthly matters, readers should understand that I am describing a fictional example for the sake of understanding only. Such an attitude would be impossible within the spiritual circle of luminous beings, because it would cause the destruction of the Luminary's own spiritual organism.

⁂

Pupils on the path to the radiant, eternal Spirit can only hope to succeed in their efforts if they regard all aspects of their companions' mortal, physical nature with kindheartedness and understanding—regardless of whether those fellow seekers be close friends or complete strangers. They must come to realize that although each person's mortal nature may differ, the *spiritual* organism that their companions seek to become conscious of is of the very same substance as their own.

Similarly, it should be evident that in the realm of the Spirit, one cannot attain that which one seeks for oneself while negating it for others.

We are concerned here with treasures that are not the same for each person, but are completely equal with regard to origin and quality.

Those who would wish to deny another person these spiritual riches will only deprive themselves.

Now that I have described what must be avoided, let me point out what is required.

To be sure, a unified consciousness that integrates the intellect, the spirit and the soul is a necessary precondition for those who wish to experience the realm of radiant Spirit. This does not mean, however, that there should simply be a change in the content of one's intellectual thought, so that only matters concerning the spirit and the soul now occupy the mind.

Rather, we are dealing here with three distinct types of consciousness, each of which imparts a different aspect of experience, and these are all intended to become integrated within one supreme consciousness—the divine spark within the individual, which is experienced as the eternal "I."

A great deal, therefore, depends upon the willingness of human beings to experience entirely new forms of consciousness—forms that have very little in common with the consciousness of the mind with which we are familiar. These new forms of consciousness cannot be described in words and can only be truly understood as they unfold within the self.

Those who seek the Spirit will not advance in the slightest if they now set out to form a mental construct of this state of consciousness, as a way of understanding that which is as yet unknown to them, and which they will experience upon awakening to the radiant, eternal Spirit and the timeless energies of the soul.

All that is required of pupils so that they may progress on the path to the Spirit can be accomplished in this tangible, physical world, although the effects of their efforts in this world reach far beyond, into the regions of the soul and the radiant Spirit.

ALL PUPILS HAVE the obligation to at all times conduct themselves with a dignity that is worthy of their spiritual nature, both as regards their fellow companions on the path and with the outside world—even if that spiritual nature is only still latent within them.

The moment individuals resolve to become pupils of the Spirit in order to become conscious of the eternal soul that lives within their spiritual organism, and to awaken to the timeless realm of the Spirit, they must willingly withdraw from all pursuits their fellow human beings may engage in but which might stand in the way of, or even make impossible, the unfolding of their spiritual organism. The need for such a stance is self-evident and no formal vow is needed to confirm it.

One has only to look at the pleasure-seeking pursuits of our time to see endless examples of how the "highly refined" human animal engages in activities that sabotage the attainment of consciousness within the realm of Spirit. And even in more serious areas of life human beings engage in many practices so primitive that they barely even reach the level of the animal soul.

Those who wish to understand me, will understand me.

Seekers of the Spirit should not try to do battle with such behaviors but, rather, should simply turn aside from them and try, as much as possible, to distance themselves from all that is vulgar and demeaning to life and behave instead in ways worthy of the eternal Spirit. They must never tire of demonstrating to others, through their own example, which pursuits are beneficial to their inner life and which are detrimental.

But here I must urge you to please not misunderstand me!

I have no regard for those who repudiate behaviors incompatible with striving towards the

Spirit but who cannot bring lightness and a sense of humor to their efforts.

A disapproving, aloof attitude, grumbling, and arguing are poor methods for opening the eyes of others so that they may come to realize that they are slaves to their over-stimulated nervous systems and to their own clueless assumptions as to what is right for them.

More effective than all else is the influence imparted by setting an example. As regards their fellow human beings, the most important task of those who seek to reach the realm of radiant Spirit is to lead the way through their own exemplary behavior.

A single inspiring act can be more instructive than hours of discussion and debate. The more pupils of the Spirit understand the impact their actions have on others—whether they reach few or many people—the more valuable their influence can be.

Pupils on the Spirit's path must understand that they are lost in a fog of arrogant, misguided thinking so long as they believe that winning a dispute with their companions is as valuable an achievement as conquering their own darkness.

THE PATH OF MY PUPILS

Not through words, but only through actions, do pupils prove that they have achieved victory within themselves.

CHAPTER EIGHT

INNER LIFE AND OUTER WORLD

I believe I have made it sufficiently clear that those who seek for truth within may only consider themselves to be "my" pupils insofar as they are guided in their own strivings by what I have taught in my books. They should not see anything more in my person than someone who is qualified to set down what has been written; I am merely the mediator and presenter of the insights and guidance that have been clearly and thoroughly discussed in my writings.

When I speak of someone as my pupil I am describing a purely *spiritual* relationship, in which I bear responsibility through all eternity for those individuals who apply my teachings in the way I have described and have therefore truly earned the right to be considered as my pupils.

THE PATH OF MY PUPILS

This relationship should not be equated with the sense of responsibility that is felt and spoken of by conscientious pastors of various religious congregations towards their "flock." Rather, my responsibility for those who precisely follow my guidance on the "path that leads into the Spirit" is an unbreakable commitment that will endure even after death, when they abide in states of existence other than their former mortal state, and will bring with it demands that do not cease until those who trusted in my teachings have each and every one attained what I have promised them.

However, I must ask readers of my books to clearly differentiate between those experiences I describe that are spiritually possible for every human being and those heights that may be reached only in rare circumstances, when certain prerequisites are met. These latter experiences I only describe in order to delineate all the levels of spiritual experiences that exist, although these highest levels are, without question, not attainable by every human being during life on earth and are to be contrasted with that which I would like every pupil of the Spirit to attain.

I allow my pupils to glimpse, in the most vivid way, these highest levels of inner development, still unattainable for them here on earth, so that they may better orient themselves and understand their own position within the vast realm of the Spirit. However, this does not mean I can promise that they themselves may attain this level of development.

Each level I have defined as being attainable calls for a successively greater degree of development of the spiritual organism. I describe what one must already have achieved within in order to ascend to the next level of spiritual experience.

After a thoughtful reading of my texts, pupils will be able to determine exactly where they stand. They must take care, however, to not reinterpret the characteristics of a given level of experience, that I have described so clearly, in their own favor.

In matters of this world, one may sometimes feign a level of accomplishment such that others will believe one truly has attained it. But in the life of the Spirit, every false claim to

THE PATH OF MY PUPILS

have achieved a higher level of accomplishment than one truly has will fail mercilessly because those who are so ready to deceive only deceive themselves.

The spiritual level that individuals have actually attained is determined solely by the degree to which they are able to experience the eternal realm of radiant Spirit.

It should be clear to all that we are not dealing here with steps, as one might climb upon a ladder, or clearly defined states that can be ranked or ordered in a fixed and rigid manner.

I have learned, however, that such a misunderstanding does indeed exist. Time and again, I have had the experience of pupils wanting me to number the steps on Jacob's ladder for them.

And so I say to them these words:

Only that which is of the spirit can become conscious of spirit.

Spirit may only be experienced through union with it and that which would unite with Spirit must itself be of the Spirit.

INNER LIFE AND OUTER WORLD

To the Spirit, everything that is not of the Spirit is not real—it does not exist.

I am speaking here of the eternal, radiant, indestructible, timeless Spirit—not about anything having to do with the product of mortal minds.

Human beings could never enter the Spirit's realm if they were made up only of that which can be apprehended by the physical senses.

Only because mortal, human beings are, at the same time, eternal, spiritual substance can they—upon uniting with the Spirit's life—become truly conscious of the spirit of Eternity that lives within their being.

For this consciousness to come about, one must maintain a certain kind of bearing in relation to the world and within one's self, and go forward with patient perseverance.

My teachings describe in great detail the various ways in which the needed bearing may be cultivated.

The first and foremost purpose of cultivating this inner bearing is to learn to live one's life with full consciousness, to become inwardly alive and to gradually shed the habit of living mainly in one's thoughts.

A life that is conscious and alive should take the place of a life lived in the mind.

This transformation will be complete when even one's thoughts are *lived* rather than merely "thought."

I am unable to say any more clearly what is meant by this. I am certain, though, that none of those still accustomed to "thinking" their lives can even faintly imagine what I mean here.

Nor is it necessary that they do so—because the essential task is not imagining but, rather, learning to *live*.

Those who "think" their lives believe that thinking is living, and that, because their mental life is active, they experience life in its fullness. For such individuals life is merely material for thought—even though life actually *encompasses* all the sources of thought-life that exist. Such thought-life is extinguished the moment thought itself ceases to be.

Still, life can nevertheless be *reduced* to thought and countless millions experience life only in their thoughts. But the radiant spirit of Eternity can never be grasped in thought, only by living life itself—as an experience within the *self* and not an experience that is within the mind.

When life is merely thought, it only has reality through thoughts. Whereas, truly living is a never-ending, ever-unfolding event in which one is immersed fully and completely.

Learning to truly live is the task of all who wish to find their way into the Spirit's realm. One does not enter life within the Spirit by *thinking* life but, rather, through a sublime inner experience that only those are able to experience who immerse themselves in life— those who live their lives with full engagement where others merely live in their own thoughts.

THIS TASK OF learning to live cannot be accomplished overnight nor does the ability to truly live life come upon a human being as a sudden illumination, as if out of nowhere.

It is an accomplishment that one must work for.

It is a kind of learning that entirely bypasses the intellect and, as with all learning, has its levels of accomplishment—or, if one wishes to stay with the metaphor of an inner path, stations along the way.

The masters of the Art of Living have in every age spoken of successive "stages" or "way stations" in order to convey the sequential nature of progress on the inner path to seekers who as yet are not fully alive. However, one should not take this to mean there are a set of rigidly determined stages that form some kind of methodology for the attainment of enlightenment.

When I speak of being "fully alive" I am not speaking here of the body's biological processes, commonly referred to as life by those who as yet "live" only in thought and mental comprehension.

In the place of a path or the steps of a staircase or ladder, one might choose the image of a living tree to better illustrate how, during this process of learning what it is to be alive, each stage of growth evolves and is transformed into the one that follows, over the course of years.

I may, of course, describe the growth of this tree, and the process of learning to become fully alive, using any number of different analogies. But although the concept of discrete stages may allow one to better understand the gradual and sequential nature of such progress, each type of description could easily be replaced by another way of organizing the steps involved.

The process of advancing on the path is not changed in any way whether I divide it into seven, seventy-seven, or seven thousand way stations, stages or steps.

One cannot therefore say that a person has attained step number seventy or some such but only that this person is only just at the beginning, or quite far, or very far along.

The grading system that is used in Freemasonry and similar fraternal orders, in which the grade one has achieved is similar to a military rank, is not relevant here.

All ways of describing the path other than the one I have put forth are nonsense.

THE PATH OF MY PUPILS

"Nonsense" because they are lacking in all sense and do not correspond to reality.

I state this here as clearly as possible because some of my pupils do not seem to be quite convinced.

※

I AM NOT PRESENTING theories wherein B is the result of A and C follows from B. Rather, I speak of my own living experiences.

It has been many years since I merely "thought" my life and now I truly live it—and I live my thoughts as well.

I was not granted any special favor as I pursued my path; on the contrary, the path I myself was obliged to follow in order to learn to live was incomparably more intense and difficult than would be possible for any student of mine to travel.

Nothing was ever handed to me on a "silver platter."

This kind of learning never ends because it must be practiced without ceasing.

The ability to live one's thoughts survives even death. The death of the physical body has bearing on the practice of living life only insofar as human beings in eternal life cannot live their thoughts unless they first learned to live them while still in a physical body.

Those who did not learn to live their thoughts while still in the physical body, will, after death, only be able to think their thoughts as if in a dream. So too, they will only be able to experience themselves through dream-like thought, though these thoughts will no longer be registered in a physical brain. And this dream state will continue until they learn to come alive and fully live themselves within the realm of radiant Spirit.

※

It is for good reason that I speak of an organism composed of spiritual substance.

I use the term "organism" to refer to something that has grown out of itself and has life that issues from its own being.

The physical body, by contrast, is not an organism in this sense but is instead an interdependent system of organs.

I am aware that one may use different terminology to describe the same concepts and during the days when I still thought my life, I too made use of the usual types of terminology. But since I have begun to live my thoughts, I no longer have need of such terminology.

Still, my pupils are at liberty to "translate" everything that I have said into language and terms that are familiar to them.

I do not want my pupils to feel rigidly bound to my words; what I intend is that they should not simply let my words lie static on the printed page but, rather, allow them to move and transform.

I MUST ALSO tell my pupils why I am, unfortunately, duty bound to refer to myself so often in my books—although nothing is more difficult for me than to even hear myself called by name here in life on earth.

Yet, I must proceed without regard for my personal desires and inclination, for the following two reasons:

Firstly, I am obliged by the Spirit—to my own, not insignificant distress—to identify myself to those who read my words—to show my credentials, as it were—whether I wish to do so or not and regardless of how I may feel about how my words are received.

In other words, I am obligated by the Spirit to give my readers insight into how I came to write my books.

Secondly, I am closest to my own experience and know it as no other can, and am thus able to regulate and direct it.

I know myself to be absolutely free of ego, even when I examine the most hidden places within me. I am accustomed, far more than other human beings, to view myself with sober objectivity. For this reason, I am my own best resource for learning, through inner dialogue with myself, how to express the things I have experienced so as to make them understandable to others.

No one who knows me even superficially could ever entertain the foolish thought that I have made myself the subject of my writings because I am enamored of my own person. My person is my *servant* and, as such, is in constant service to me so that I may carry out the duties required of me by the Spirit.

Had I the inclination to indulge in narcissistic vanities, I would surely know ways to do so that would be more pleasant—for I am no ascetic and the curious proclivity of ascetics to seek out and enjoy what causes them pain is alien to me.

Just as I can truly say that I am not trying to "find myself" in my endeavors, I must also clearly state that the motivation for my tireless efforts is not solely to guide my pupils on the path to eternal salvation but, also, to release the creative energies they need to build their lives on earth.

To be sure, my pupils will have to clearly distinguish between that which I can bring into being by way of the Spirit on their behalf, and what they must do themselves, in their daily lives.

Life in the Spirit is by no means incompatible with life in the everyday world and those who seek to awaken to the Spirit must first learn to master the challenges of daily life.

One should not heed those dreamy, unrealistic types who in every age have taught that the spirit of Eternity can only be touched if those who seek it turn their backs on everything in earthly life. Quite the opposite is true. This earthly life is a reflection of Reality and, thus, if one denies it one denies Reality.

Those who seek the Spirit should not cling so closely to the earth that they cannot rise above it. On the other hand, they must always bear in mind that everything in this earthly realm is encompassed by the Eternal.

The energies that emanate from the Eternal realm are transformed many times, and only their final result is experienced in the outer, physical world, as these forces act upon each other and react in a reflexive manner. Even so, mortal human beings are given more than simply shadows and empty appearances.

Those individuals whose spiritual senses are sufficiently developed are able to trace all earthly phenomena back to the point at which perception with one's physical senses ends and perception with one's spiritual senses begins. It is here that the primal forces which cause all form to *be* are experienced as radiant, spiritual substance.

Thus the outermost is connected to the innermost in a continuum of *being*. That which manifests in form as "outermost" is already too near the region that is eternally immobile —the absolute "nothing"—so that it can never enter into the "innermost" which abides in unfathomable, eternal motion and is absolutely free.

Because mortal humans are in their essence beings of the innermost Reality who have become lost in the outermost of worlds, they can only hope to regain consciousness of their innermost if they begin from the point at which they now find themselves—namely from their own physical bodies and the outer world in which they live.

Human beings become conscious of this outer world through their physical senses and all changes in their state of being are perceived through their ability to feel.

All things in the environment that surrounds one's physical body can be sensed only to the extent that they have an effect on the physical body—regardless of whether such effects are barely perceptible or intense, pleasant or painful.

All such sense perceptions are felt only for a moment and are soon replaced by new sensations, although the stringing together of such moments may create the impression of uninterrupted sensation, just as the many individual, projected images in a filmstrip are perceived by the viewer as one continuous image.

A memory of these past sensations that originated in the external world and have left their impression on the physical body is preserved for a limited time—at most until the death of the body. This memory includes the emotional content and tone of these impressions.

BEYOND THESE sensory impressions, the individual's relationship with the outer world is created and perceived solely within the imagination. However, because the products of imagination are so much subject to the human will—will in the form of *belief*—philosophers have wrongly concluded that all physical phenomena are products of the imagination.

This is certainly not the case. Rather, the products of the imagination are the result of our ability to conceptualize—to form into images—the effects of primal forces that cannot be perceived by human senses. The ability to conceptualize is a way of adapting and abbreviating, as it were, complicated processes and formulating them in such a way that they may be understood by the human mind. Despite this ability to conceptualize, the realm of imagination is not at all the same as the tangible, physical world that is accessible to the senses.

However firmly anchored in reality individuals may consider their conceptual world to be, there will at times be moments when they realize they are very far from having used their physical senses to the fullest.

The world of the imagination is, without a doubt, the greatest single factor in determining the individual's experience. This is so regardless of how little it, in fact, corresponds to the world that could be comprehended by the physical senses were the potential of these senses fully used.

INNER LIFE AND OUTER WORLD

THIS WORLD of self-created images and concepts, which holds such significant and far-reaching consequences for human life, is a very variable structure. It shifts and changes form as it is influenced not only by one's own insights and experiences but also by the imaginary worlds of others.

Thus, human beings group themselves with others who see the world as they do. This commonality of views then provides them with the "proof" that their understanding of the world is the correct one. This is so even if it is in fact only a caricature of the real world—which can only be accurately perceived if the physical senses are not blinded.

Pupils of the Spirit must therefore constantly examine their own conceptual world view and also that of the groups they have joined with and those into which life and circumstance have placed them. This may include the ethnic group into which they were born and the many sub-groups within it.

The demands of the Spirit are the same for the individual as for the many individuals within a group. Those who wish to enter into the Spirit's realm cannot meet those demands and, at the same time, adhere without question to the world view of a group whose actions and stance automatically block the inner path.

※

One cannot comprehend the universality of the eternal Spirit and believe that one can enter into its radiance while at the same time disdaining, hating, or persecuting anything; for everything belongs to and forms part of the Spirit's world. To believe otherwise is insane.

All humans carry within them the Spirit's radiance, even if it be in latent form. Therefore one must carefully distinguish between the rejection of other people's opinions or positions, which are rooted in their animal nature, and the devaluation of the persons themselves. It is arrogance and an affront to Spirit to spurn those who differ from ourselves in their views and beliefs; be they individuals, groups, nations or races.

※

It should be self-evident that harboring feelings of hate will cause one to become blind and deaf to the radiance of the Spirit's realm.

INNER LIFE AND OUTER WORLD

By no means, however, should one seek to eradicate the capacity to feel hate because then also the capacity to feel love—the eternal, primal force that is the essence of the Spirit—would be extinguished. Feelings of hate should be calmly and dispassionately observed as they arise and intensify—but should not be nourished. The pupil on the Spirit's path must then begin the noble and essential task of transforming the hate, just now felt in full intensity, into love—the opposite pole of the self-same energy.

Wherever hatred against individuals, groups or other ethnicities is considered to be justified and is allowed to grow there can be no inner development for pupils of the Spirit. Should pupils find themselves in such environments, it will behoove them to leave any positions they hold or that are offered to them to those who are content to live according to their animal nature, and have no wish to rise above it.

Whatever influences seekers may be facing from the outside world, they must always bear in mind that nothing in this outer world can block their path into the Spirit, so long as they diligently follow the guidance I have so abundantly provided in my books.

Progress on the inner path will come from *applying* my guidance in daily life—and nothing will be gained by simply agreeing enthusiastically with my words.

※

Pupils who strive to live in accordance with my teaching must first create order in their everyday lives.

Only when everything in their daily lives has been ordered in every respect—only then have those who seek the Spirit earned the right to continue on their path and only then are they entitled to expect that they will actually attain the fullness of all that is possible for them in the realm of Spirit during this life.

An easy-going attitude towards life, in which everyday matters are regarded as trivial and not worthy of full attention on the noble path towards the Eternal—although popular and widespread—is always detrimental to the goal.

Even if something is indeed a trifle, what is no trifle is the manner in which it is handled—

whether it is dealt with in a manner compatible with the requirements of the Spirit.

In the Gospels we read the parable of the faithful steward, in which the master praises him as follows: "Well done, thou good and faithful servant: thou has been faithful over a few things, I will make thee ruler over many things." (Matthew 25:21 King James Version)

What is being shown in this parable is nothing less than one of the most essential requirements of the Spirit.

Those who cannot manage to conduct themselves in their transitory time on earth in such a way that their thoughts, words, and deeds may be acceptable to the Spirit, have failed to understand how their life in the world around them should be used to bring them closer to their goal, and all their striving to gain consciousness of the eternal Spirit will be of no use whatsoever.

Those who will consistently regard every decision in their everyday lives, no matter how small, no matter how hurried, as if their eternal salvation depended on it are far nearer to becoming conscious in the Spirit than they might suppose. Even if their inherited traits stand in the way of a full inner unfolding during their life on earth, they nevertheless will enter Eternity with a self that is conscious of the Spirit.

※

F<small>EW THINGS</small> have been so misunderstood by individuals throughout human history—in every corner of the earth and at all levels of civilization—as the nature of the radiant, eternal Spirit as it stirs within them.

Those who seek the Spirit have often been misled, in past times and still today, by a simplistic type of thinking which posits that our mortal, everyday existence, experienced with the physical senses, must certainly be abhorrent to the Spirit.

Because of this belief, many people conclude that it must be impossible to become conscious in the Spirit's realm unless one regards this mortal life with scorn and a measure of contempt.

One can easily count the few who have been able to overcome this disabling belief, inherited from by-gone times, and who have, instead, come to understand that the path into the radiant Spirit begins in their present life, here in the midst of this seemingly insignificant, everyday world.

Only those who are able to cast away the dead weight of past ideas and arrive at this fundamental insight may become pupils of the Spirit.

CHAPTER NINE

HOW ONE OUGHT TO USE MY BOOKS

Shortly after the turn of the century, I made my first attempts to put down in words spiritual insights which had come to me through my own living experience of the Spirit's reality. I wrote in a secret code, invented by me, in order to protect the sacredness of that which I was committing to paper from any profanation. But even a decade later, when my conscious experience of the Spirit as well as my attempts to describe this in words had become familiar and natural for me, I never in my wildest dreams thought that I would publish my writings for all the world to see.

I decided on the following arrangement: I would, at the appropriate time, leave the "key" to my secret code in the hands of an individual who appeared trustworthy to me and this person would have the task of publishing what

THE PATH OF MY PUPILS

I had written in a suitable manner, after my death.

For years there had also been a "testamentary disposition" and a copy of the "key" in a sealed envelope lying among my papers, in case I died suddenly, before I could appoint my trustworthy executor.

Never did I imagine that one day I, myself, would make my "legacy" public and that I would be the one to transcribe for the typesetter that which I had so carefully set down in a code understandable only by me.

During a visit by the spiritual guide and teacher most important to me—who had become the primary authority I looked to in such matters—he for the first time offered me clear, convincing reasons why my task would not be fulfilled by simply leaving my teachings behind after I died. Instead, it was my duty to publish these teachings during my lifetime and to appear before the entire world as their representative and author. Upon learning of this, I fell for a long time into an unspeakable depression as, day after day, I sought to find some way of reconciling the necessity of revealing my innermost self to everyone with my deep need for seclusion and isolation, so fundamental to my spiritual nature.

I managed to wrest myself from such inner torments only after the same fatherly spiritual guide, whom I loved with deep veneration, met with me again. This meeting took place far from home, during a year of spiritual and artistic work I was pursuing in Greece—at which time I was also to meet other men whose spiritual brother I should henceforth become.

It was from Athens that I sent the first small manuscript entitled "The Light from Himavat" —signed only with the first three letters of the spiritual name conferred on me by my teachers and brothers—to a limited public, in order to gauge the response.

This occurred in the year 1913.

The reception of this small, instructional booklet was far better than I had expected.

The text of this booklet was taken from *The Book on the Royal Art*, which had not yet been published, and was incorporated into that book once again when it was published.

※

AFTER THIS initial trial publication, not a year passed without the publication of at least one of these concise booklets, or the simultaneous publication of several of them, and readers did not know whether to admire my voluminous productivity or to include me among the legions of authors who simply churn out books.

No one could have known that much of what was published in such rapid succession had already been lying locked away in my writing desk for years, almost ready for publication, or had been written in Greece long before being made public.

These works include: almost everything in *The Book on the Living God* and *The Book on Human Nature*, almost everything in *More Light* and *The Book on the Royal Art* and parts of *The Book of Dialogues*, as well as writings originally intended to be published after my death, that I had to alter so that certain passages would make sense when published during my lifetime.

HOW ONE OUGHT TO USE MY BOOKS

Once I had become convinced that the task with which I had been charged also included the duty to make public everything I had written in my books, already during my lifetime, it became clear to me that it would be impossible to fulfill this obligation in the form of a spiritual legacy as I had previously planned.

I mention these things here because at times I have encountered those who consider my books to be "literature," a categorization quite removed from the actual facts.

I have never been driven by even the slightest literary ambition.

It has always been the heaviest of burdens for me to write the things I write, which by their very nature resist being put into words. It is a responsibility most difficult to bear, and one I would gladly have rid myself of, were it only possible to do so.

I DO NOT WRITE because I enjoy it.

Nothing that I have written up until this very hour has been easy to write. Such ease could never have been possible because the almost unbearable eternal responsibility, which cannot be lifted from my shoulders, requires me to examine every sentence, every word and syllable, with the greatest care, so as to determine whether it is suitable to carry the content entrusted to it. I do not mean suitable in a literary sense but, rather, in the sense of whether the chosen words are able to be carriers of the spiritual substance that I wish to offer through these words.

Wherever necessary the sentences, words and syllables I have chosen are "charged," as it were, with substance of the radiant Spirit.

I can neither describe nor teach this process by which words are infused with spiritual substance—and which is "magic" in the highest sense of the word. I can only point out that what I do is in no way mysterious but is, rather, a matter of making use of the spiritual vibrations latent in almost all elements of language, which are released when spoken out loud or even only just thought.

Many have felt the high help emanating from these vibrations, without understanding its source—the spiritual energy accumulated in the words offered to them.

HOW ONE OUGHT TO USE MY BOOKS

In order to describe the uncommon process by which I create my writings, I have had to overcome a great deal of most understandable reticence, knowing that my words would encounter a complete lack of understanding by much of the reading public. It should, however, be evident from my explanation how my books should *not* be used.

One should not read my books as one would read something more or less interesting, fantastical, curious, or even familiar. One should not "read" them in the way most people are inclined to read these days—that is, swallowing entire groups of sentences at a glance, skimming over the text so that one hardly even reads one entire sentence, the mind "flying about," constantly someplace other than absorbing the meaning of the words before one.

One should not read my books while holding onto preconceived ideas or conventional ways of understanding.

My obligations to the radiant Spirit often make it necessary for me to use the familiar elements of language in quite unfamiliar ways because rhythm, the interval between the repetition of vowels or consonants, and similar matters are not just required for stylistic, but also for spiritual, reasons. And this, completely apart from the fact that I must, of course, permit myself to arrange the words and form the sentences so that when I read them they express to me what I wish to convey to other human beings.

It would otherwise be impossible for me to judge whether I have fulfilled the task accorded to me.

In order to genuinely absorb what is given in my books one must learn to read them with focused concentration.

Such a manner of reading will prove most worthwhile.

※

At the very first reading one should not concern oneself with anything but the general content—in the same way that the hurried reader who "never has any time" might do.

Once pupils have absorbed the contents of a particular book and satisfied their curiosity, they may then read it again in a different spirit, one which will stir a joyful resonance in their spiritual organism and eternal soul.

HOW ONE OUGHT TO USE MY BOOKS

As long as a passage in one of my books that deals with the substantial realm of the Spirit of Eternity and life within the radiant Spirit does not yet awaken a joyful echo within the reader—as if something once loved and long forgotten is now called to mind once more—then the passage in question has not been truly understood.

It is of no use, however, to now brood over such a passage or, even worse, to attempt to artificially evoke a resonant response if it does not arise spontaneously within.

Such an attempt would only feed the most harmful sort of self-deception.

If this feeling of recognition, which will impart to you an immediate sense of inner certainty and touch a wellspring of deep joy within you, is not yet present, then let the particular passage be and turn to another which at that moment speaks to you.

Pupils must return to the same book countless times if it is to give them all it has to offer.

It would be a mistake, however, if one took it into one's head to force oneself to read and re-read a particular book until it has seemingly rendered everything it has to offer.

Not only would seekers achieve nothing, they would also inwardly blunt themselves to such an extent that they would only be able to read one of my books with a receptive spirit and benefit from it after years at best.

Rest assured that it was not an arbitrary decision on my part to publish the teachings that I have been obliged to make known in small, self-contained books.

And if I refer to one of these short publications as a "book" this is a fitting description, for its contents could far more easily have been expressed in greater length and detail instead of the compact form I felt would benefit the reader.

Those who examine things a little more closely will see that it would certainly not have been difficult to expand the contents of such compact publications and turn them into thick volumes. They will also discover that not only did I have good reasons for offering all of my teachings to the humanity of our day—which is so often "too busy" to read—in books whose scope and length I was concerned to keep to a minimum but also that the particular selections I chose are justified on psychological grounds.

If one wants to teach one's fellow human beings about one's personal, perhaps quite unconventional, understandings of metaphysical matters, then this can certainly be accomplished with a single book that could either be of modest size or grow to the size of an encyclopedic volume without gaining or losing in value.

However, if I am to guide those who wish to become conscious of their innate spiritual nature in such a way that they will truly find what they are seeking, then I must consider which approaches are most suited to each seeker's ability to absorb what I wish to convey, and a great many other factors. Therefore, I can only be of help if I offer many different perspectives on the sublime goal so earnestly sought.

Similarly, I must advise my pupils to immediately select a different book if the teachings and imagery of the book they are reading does not evoke a deep resonance within. Indeed, they should not hesitate to try different books until they find the one which is able to evoke such an inner response.

We cannot absorb the same content with the same depth at any given time.

Different ways of saying the same thing are needed at different times. And often we need to view the source we look to for our guidance from different perspectives, so that we may more clearly see the way to satisfy our wish to experience that which we have not yet experienced.

Because I continually search for new ways to describe things concerning the Spirit, and because I teach my pupils to view these things from every possible perspective, they will never be at a loss as to which one of my books to select at a given moment.

I caution my pupils, however, to consider each of my books as separate unto itself, and not to mix what I write in one of my books with the content of my other books.

HOW ONE OUGHT TO USE MY BOOKS

Everything in my books can be made to harmonize with all the rest but, right from the beginning, I never deemed it absolutely necessary to express what I wish to convey using exactly the same words in each book. Such a limitation would have forced me to leave too much unsaid about matters that are close to my heart and which I dearly wanted to make known, once I realized how badly those who seek the Spirit needed to hear them.

Since I did not intend to present a system or world-view in my books, and often desired to present particular experiences as distinct accounts—separate from experiences I have described in other writings—misunderstandings could easily arise if the manner of expression in one book were mixed with that of another.

WHEN READ WITH deeper insight, one can sense the profound harmony that unifies all my writings, even if in certain respects each one differs in emphasis.

The most important consideration in approaching my books always remains the same:

whether to regard them as "reading material" or as a means, tried and tested by many, to enter the path that leads one into the Spirit.

My books are intended to be guides that show seekers how they can find their way into the Spirit.

The motivation that inspires me to write has never had anything to do with wanting or hoping to be recognized as a writer by other writers.

I have always been far too concerned about the purpose to which I committed myself in writing my books to consider this sort of thing worth taking into account.

❧

Truly, I cannot work miracles and even if I could, I would not do so, because even my wish for a miracle could not be reconciled with the structure of the radiant, eternal Spirit —known to me through my direct experience.

I cannot work miracles despite all that I have included in my books. It is not enough to pick up one of my books now and then and leaf through it, simply to ponder some passage for a while.

In order for these books to offer all they have to offer, they must become my pupils' constant companions.

Not a day should be allowed to pass without reading them.

This is all the more necessary for the simple reason that today's seekers find themselves in a time and in an environment which is focused on penetrating and dominating the outer world, while they must try to preserve their focus on that which is innermost.

THE PRESENT DAY is neither better nor worse than any other period in history.

Today's world is in every respect an expression of what human beings of this time need to pass through if there is to be a reversal of the centuries-old focus on the external and a turning towards the inner world.

One should not imagine that such a reversal will be a kind of mass "conversion."

That which is truly ready for transformation will be quietly and imperceptibly transformed. Thus, we are today already in the midst of this transformation even though most people still believe the trend will be to focus ever more outward and to probe ever deeper into the realm of matter.

Most people at this time are still gazing outward, their eyes searching for far-away horizons that they long for and imagine to exist, distant from their inner selves. They cannot yet see clearly or discern how forced their striving to continue probing ever outward has become—because it is the final spasm of a universal human impulse whose energy has already long been drawn back into the source from which it flowed.

Just as fading candlelight flares up brightly just before it dies, today's triumphant accomplishments that people extoll as evidence of the vitality of the outward drive are nothing other than confirmations of its inevitable demise—because the reversal in direction has already begun, quietly and imperceptibly, wherever the necessary preconditions have been fulfilled.

The great, universal human impulses may bend the arc of these striving energies, but cannot break their force.

⁂

IN SUCH A TIME of turning, each person's thoughts, deeds, and words are especially important, far more so than at those times when the domination by outward-directed impulses is not yet near its end.

At such times, those who seek the center of their being in the realm of Spirit have need—more than anyone else—of an inner world of experience in which that which is yet to be born in the outer world of the future is already alive with transformative power within them, shaped in a way that reflects Reality.

The first and foremost purpose of my books is to help those who seek the Spirit open this realm of experience within themselves.

My books can only accomplish this purpose, however, if those who consult them seek their counsel day-by-day, keeping in mind the fact, proven a thousand times over, that their contents can never be exhausted.

I can confidently say that they would not see the day on which my books had nothing new to say to them, even if it were possible for them to live many centuries in their mortal bodies and spend every day in close communion with my books.

※

In a time when those outward-directed impulses that have driven human activity are in the process of reversing, much that is thought to be progressive and determinative of the future is in truth only the residue of the desire to cling to the past.

For this reason seekers are in constant danger of being deceived if they are not able to access the insights that shed light on that which will truly form the future.

Such insights they will find on almost every page of my books.

If they daily seek the counsel of my books, the future will reveal itself in their present life and, because they have come to know it in advance, they will become co-creators of that which is to come.

HOW ONE OUGHT TO USE MY BOOKS

Only then will they discover that their existence on this earth can never lose its meaning—even in the saddest and most trying times. They will know that this meaning is not to be found in the realm of thought—their own thoughts or what the minds of others have created—but, rather, in their ability to shape their actions so that they may fulfill that which the Spirit wants from them.

Those who would be my pupils should not believe it is enough to think like me or to suppose they think like me. They become my pupils at the moment that they transform their lives in accordance with the guidance in my books.

If one day they can say that these books motivated them to begin a new a life filled with inner certainty and a hitherto unknown joy in being active and alive, and that they would no longer want to live without the teachings and suggestions I have given them—then they have used my books just as they ought to be used.

⁂

JUST AS WITH all things of this world, books do not become a blessing or a curse solely because of what is written in them, but more so because of how they are used.

Thus, the spiritual help which my books can release depends to a large extent on the way they are used by the reader.

Everything that exists on earth can be misused—there is no thing that cannot be robbed of its potential to bestow blessings.

My books are no exception.

Those who cannot yet understand how to use these books correctly would do better to lay them aside until such time as they find themselves able to use them in the way they are intended to be used.

So long as the striving for clarity and light remains alive in them—they will not wait in vain.

Only those individuals who, after honestly examining their conscience, may claim that they are truly of good will, will find inner peace through the use of my books.

REMINDER

"Yet here I must point out again that if one would derive the fullest benefit from studying the books I wrote to show the way into the Spirit, one has to read them in the original; even if this should require learning German.

"Translations can at best provide assistance in helping readers gradually perceive, even through the spirit of a different language, what I convey with the resources of my mother tongue."

From "Answers to Everyone" (1933), *Gleanings*. Bern: Kobersche Verlagsbuchhandlung, 1990

For a deeper understanding
of the core of Bô Yin Râ's teachings
you may want to read:

*The Book on the Living God,
The Book on Life Beyond* and
The Book on Human Nature

These three books should be
read together.

A description of all three books follows.

The Book on the Living God

The Book on the Living God describes the inner path that leads to birth of the Living God within--what we must do and what to avoid on the long journey towards awakening the consciousness of our timeless self.

Ordinary consciousness, Bô Yin Râ tells us, is actually like sleep; there is a greater consciousness that is alive in us, informing every cell, and our task is to unite it with our self-awareness.

We must also set aside the ideas we have been taught about an anthropomorphic God. God is not meant to be an external object of worship but, rather, an experience to be awakened within us. We are cautioned to avoid the pitfalls that might divert us: following false teachers or believing that certain foods or exercises, or ecstatic experiences, have spiritual merit. Everyday life, when lived with attention to the ultimate goal, will lead us towards a gradual awakening of our timeless self.

E.W.S. Publisher

Contents: Word of Guidance. "The Tabernacle of God is with Men." The White Lodge. Meta-Physical Experiences. The Inner Journey. The En-Sof. On Seeking God. On Leading an Active Life. On "Holy Men" and "Sinners." The Hidden Side of Nature. The Secret Temple. Karma. War and Peace. The Unity among Religions. The Will to Find Eternal Light. The Human Being's Higher Faculties of Knowing. On Death. On the Spirit's Radiant Substance. The Path toward Perfection. On Everlasting Life. The Spirit's Light Dwells in the East. Faith, Talismans, and Images of God. The Inner Force in Words. A Call from Himavat. Giving Thanks. Epilogue.

The Book on Life Beyond

The Book on Life Beyond is a guide to help readers understand what they can expect to find in the life beyond death, and how to best prepare for it.

Bô Yin Râ explains that life beyond is actually another dimension of the same life we know here on earth—just as real and solid, but perceived through spiritual, rather than our limited, physical senses. He emphasizes the direct connection between our actions here on earth and their effects on life beyond. We bring with us into life beyond the same state of inner being with which we departed, and are able to experience its wonders exactly to the degree to which we have developed our spiritual self. For example, those who have failed to show compassion for others and have lived selfishly will find that life beyond lacks the warmth and light that other, more developed souls can perceive.

Bô Yin Râ counsels us to mentally practice the "art of dying" as a meditative practice to prepare for the transition from physical to spiritual existence. The goal is to constantly orient one's thinking, emotions and desires toward transformation of the self, in order to be able to receive the spiritual help that will be available to us after death.

E.W.S. Publisher

Contents: Introduction. The Art of Dying. The Temple of Eternity and the World of Spirit. The Only Absolute Reality. What Should One Do?

The Book on Human Nature

The Book on Human Nature presents basic concepts about human nature with the goal of inspiring readers to awaken the timeless, spiritual spark within. We become fully human only when the spiritual potential within us gradually awakens and infuses our material, purely animal selves. It is a path that every human being may and should pursue.

A central understanding is that all life results from the joining of opposites, in particular, the polarity of male and female energies. Bô Yin Râ emphasizes that the true spiritual human being is male and female united in one entity; when we seek our spiritual self, we must call forth the male and female in ourselves and in all things. He discusses the biblical fall from grace as a descent from the spiritual plane, in which male and female were united, onto a material plane, in which male and female are split apart.

Bô Yin Râ warns men that holding onto the illusion of male superiority means forfeiting their spiritual life. While the spiritual paths that are natural for men and women are different in tone—open and receptive for women, active and grasping for men—they are equal and complementary. He tells us that *true* marriage is preparation for the life beyond: by coordinating the desires, wills and attitudes of two beings we once again bring about, in some measure, the original state in which male and female energies are united.

E.W.S. Publisher

Contents: Introduction. The Mystery Enshrouding Male and Female. The Path of the Female. The Path of the Male. Marriage. Children. The Human Being of the Age to Come. Epilogue. A Final Word.

www.ingramcontent.com/pod-product-compliance
Lightning Source LLC
Chambersburg PA
CBHW022130080426
42734CB00006B/299